Wayne Palmer is from southern England, born and raised in the Southampton area in a council house. His dad was a lorry driver and mum a school cook. He left school to start a traditional engineering craft apprenticeship, but continued with his education one day a week, and in the evening, right up until he was 28 and the birth of his son. By his own confession, it makes him a late starter.

Wayne completed his apprenticeship in production engineering, specialising in turning and milling, after which he moved into technical sales and installations before moving onto junior management roles.

He started his first business, Thinking Space, in 2003, at home in his parents' dining room. This company now has international offices manufacturing in the northern and southern hemispheres and he has another three companies which he has built up, which fit nicely into the Thinking Space family. These companies represent leading brands from Europe and as well as their own brands. They see products being exported globally. Now a market leader in several sectors, 40% of the products are sold internationally.

A bad golfer and very average sailor, Wayne's passion is working with young people and trying to show them what they can achieve with hard work and common sense. Wayne believes in the apprenticeship scheme, and on-the-job training as a real alternative to university.

He also puts his success down to teamwork and talking fantastic people into working with him.

The business and this book would have been impossible without the support of a lot of people. It's a real team effort to set up and run a company from scratch and then write about it. Sally has been behind me all the way and spent hours proofreading and then asking what the hell I was talking about! So thanks to her and everyone who encouraged me to complete the book and suggest that people would want to read it!

Wayne Palmer

JAM TOMORROW

AUSTIN MACAULEY PUBLISHERS™

LONDON ∗ CAMBRIDGE ∗ NEW YORK ∗ SHARJAH

A CIP catalogue record for this title is available from the British Library.

ISBN 9781398449954 (Paperback)
ISBN 9781398449961 (ePub e-book)

www.austinmacauley.com

First Published 2022
Austin Macauley Publishers Ltd®
1 Canada Square
Canary Wharf
London
E14 5AA

This would not have been produced without the help of friends, family, and colleagues who have inspired me during my career. My two business partners, Paul Atkins and Paul Roberts, who have been with me forever, are an inspiration.

Ever present is also my sister, Tina, whose encouragement and optimism kept me chugging along.

I promise everyone that I will stop talking about this book now that it's finally finished.

Table of Contents

Who Is This Book For?

This book is aimed at anyone who likes the idea of starting something on their own but has no clue where to begin. It will highlight some of the skills which might be needed, the risks that may need to be taken and good and bad moments which may be experienced along the way. It is also aimed at anyone that is interested in a few funny stories about one bloke's experience winging it in business, and I have to admit I am still winging it today.

The reason for writing this is not to bolster my own standing or gain future business, but to educate people in a way they can all relate to. I was not an academic and did not go to university. If I can motivate just one young person to just have a go, then I will have succeeded. Given the choice, I would be happy to talk to people about this book and my own experiences at schools and more informal settings.

I am certainly not an author. I would score myself four out of ten for general English, and I am not 100% sure I know anything about grammar. I am sure this book has good content and it may have been better written by someone else, but I have to admit, I have enjoyed putting it together! I know that a lot of people enjoy hearing my stories, and like me, they are motivated by hearing about actual events and the highs and lows of a normal guy in business. Nothing here is made up, it all happened and I have only written what I believe in, so, if a few people are motivated to start something new and can avoid some of my mistakes, then it will have been worthwhile.

I hope I have written this in a way that will appeal to young people. I came from a working-class council house family and followed the apprenticeship route to work. If a semi or un-skilled person like me can achieve, then for sure, more young people can certainly give it a go in a newer world, where they have the advantages of a potential global audience and better education enhanced by the internet.

It is fair to say that some of this is not my own work. Some of the suggestions and ideas have evolved from people I have worked with and the way I have interacted with them. I do not always remember who said what, but they know who they are, so cheers.

So, why this short titles format?

For me, life is a journey. It jumps all over the place. Some bits are great, some are rubbish and things do not necessarily happen in a particular order. Everything I have written will be relevant at different times, so I wanted to create a book you could thumb through, picking out the area important to you at a specific time.

The chapter headings are to remind you of the content in a humorous way. I want them to stick with you so that you, too, can use them.

Setting up and running a company is not for everyone. Some people are just not cut out for it. If someone tells you anyone can do it, they are talking bollocks. It is not a bad thing to know where your comfort zone is and what your limitations are. What I do urge you to do is never be afraid to try. I say this to my kids every day, partly because I do believe as parents, my generation have made some basic mistakes with our kids. The so called 'snowflake' generation is our making.

These experiences have come from starting up and growing my first company, 'Thinking Space'. The company started in my parents' dining room and the house garage. The company is a manufacturing business, but the lessons learned are transferable into any sector. Over the 20 years of growth, the business now has 40 employees manufacturing on three continents and exporting globally.

I now find myself with the title of CEO and the owner of two additional companies completely unrelated to Thinking Space.

The trigger for me to start recording this stuff came after a great experience while working in the Middle East. The book started after lunch in an air traffic control tower. The experience was bizarre and I just knew I had to tell people about it. Let me get that story off my chest right now.

One of my company designs and builds technical furniture for control room desks, that house electronic equipment, that are individually made from our own aluminium extrusion system. If you are not clear what that means, imagine the air traffic control tower at an airport. Usually round, tall, and in the middle of the airfield. We design, build, and install the circular desks, which includes mounting all the technical equipment in such a way that the controller is both working efficiently and can still see out of all the windows.

This story revolves around my second visit to site. I was talking to the senior engineers about a technical re-fit to the tower control room as they were replacing some of the technology, so the old desks had to go. Many of those I was working with had been educated in the UK, so as requested, I came armed with shortbread biscuits and marmite. They were thrilled with these and after a morning's work. They asked me if I would like to join them for lunch. At which a large plastic sheet was produced and laid out on the floor. We all knelt in a small circle while one of the engineers produced a huge container of rice, which in one swift movement, he flipped upside down and slammed onto the middle of the sheet between us all. He gently pushed his hand in the rice mountain and proceeded to fill the hole with vegetable curry creating what can only be described as a curry volcano. I must say it looked fantastic with the hot watery curry seeping through the rice.

So, here I am, sitting on the floor in front of the curry volcano, dressed in a business suit and tie. What could go wrong? My main contact looks at me with a smile and asks if I would like a fork or spoon. I look around the room and see the other engineers looking at me and I said, "No, thank you." It was clearly the right answer because they all tucked in and one of the engineers proceeded to deliver the training course on how to eat with your hands.

"Wayne, take a small ball of rice in your fingertips and then use that to scoop up some of the curry and eat!" Sounded simple, and, to be fair, watching them, it could not have looked any easier. I watched a couple of times and I could see they were keen to see me have a go. I fumbled the rice into a ball only using my fingertips and then lent forward to go for some curry, immediately submerging the tip of my tie in vegetable curry. Of course, as I sat back, my tie falls back in place transferring curry to my nice, white shirt! Within five minutes, I had curry running down my arm and dripping off my elbow. I was a complete mess. There was more food on my clothes than in my mouth. I had definitely been stitched up. Before I knew it, they all had their phones out taking photos and were enjoying every second. As I continued to eat, only now with a spoon, they told me they had been working on how runny they could make a curry that still tasted good!

While we were still joking and I was trying to get myself cleaned up, a light aircraft radioed the tower to get permission to land. Without getting up from the floor, a controller reached up for the handset and told the pilot to hold as there was 'traffic' on the runway. He then tossed the handset onto the counter and continued with his lunch. Minutes passed and I was starting to worry about this aircraft when the radio sparks up again. It is the pilot, but this time there is more urgency in his voice. The controller sighs as the pilot asks if he should divert to another airport due to a lack of fuel. Our tower controller stands up, looks up and down the runway, then tells the pilot he is clear to land, and within a minute the light aircraft touches down! I was amazed this had just happened. We had delayed an aircraft from touching down because we were on lunch! Priceless.

When heading back to my hotel that evening, smelling of curry, I was thinking how did a council house boy from Hampshire end up sitting on a plastic sheet on the floor of an air traffic control tower, sharing homemade food with local people.

This story will live with me forever and makes me smile every time I think about that day. When you start a new business, you cannot always predict where your work will take you and what you will experience.

Another story that will either make you laugh or fill you with horror came when I was listing the equipment in an African air traffic control tower, so that I could produce some new layout drawings. The senior operator was with me and he was naming the items as I measured them up. The next on the list was the 'emergency' radio, which he had just picked up to chat to an incoming aircraft and which he had, in fact, been using all morning. I asked him why it was called the 'emergency' radio when they appeared to be using it for all calls. He just responded, "That's because it is an emergency, Wayne. The main radio is broken." *OK,* I thought, I could not help myself but ask another question.

"So how long has the main radio been broken?"

He smiled and said, "Um, well, about two years!"

All I could think of was, I hope the emergency radio is still working fine when I fly home!

I hope after reading this that perhaps this book is for you.

Wayne.

Chapter One
If You Want to Get There,
I Would Not Start Here!

Why would this be the first chapter? Read on.

This title always makes me smile. It refers to a statement one of my old bosses made. Michael Etherington ran a great small business based in Winchester. He was a good public speaker and was often asked to talk to colleges and universities about small business subjects. I worked for him for over ten years, learnt loads and occasionally attended one of his informal chats with young people. For me, he was an inspiration but when he came out with this line, I nearly choked on my cappuccino.

At the end of a chat to undergraduates at a local university, Michael, as usual, opened the floor up to questions. It is always my favourite bit, partly because whenever you do this, most people just want to tell you how clever they are rather than actually ask you a question. The main reason I like it so much is because every now and then, you get a gem of a statement cum question, where trying to work out how to tell someone they are an idiot without publicly humiliating them is nearly impossible.

So, a young guy stands up and asks what he is doing wrong. He has invested in a web site, made prototypes, and been trying to sell the solution for over 18 months, and despite his hardest efforts, he has not managed to sell a single unit. Michael then hit him with this line, "Sir, if you want to get there, do not start here."

He then went on to simply say, "You have come up with an idea that nobody wants!" It turns out the guy had designed an app to scan documents into your phone. His challenge was, people were simply photographing documents rather than using his idea! The number one thing you need to do is make something or provide a service that people actually want.

The most common question I am asked is, "How did you start? What was the beginning? Where was the inspiration?" This is the reason I have put this chapter first because this is the beginning of your journey. If this was a proper management training book, it would be called something like 'Market Research'. I prefer to call it doing your homework. As you read this book, you will notice that forms, documents, preparation and general detail are not my bag. This is so much more important to understand than you realise. You must know where your skills and, even more importantly, your weaknesses are. Nobody knows everything. Well, apart from my daughter when she turned 11, for a couple of years she knew bloody everything. Perhaps, she should have started a business back then! Realistically, you need to understand what skill gaps you need to fill and I will cover this in detail in another chapter. You won't know everything, so never be afraid to fail or screw up.

It started for me when I met a friend at a control room he managed. I noticed he had one of these very large 'all singing all dancing' rear projector screens at the front of it. We are talking 10m wide and 3m high. It looked amazing but was not finished. I asked him why and he said that it was not part of the services the company provided and he had not got around to looking into it. His issue was he would have to get a specialist in. The building was owned by a third party and he thought they might have an issue if he built a plasterboard wall around the screens as this would then need to be attached to a wall and may have to be fire rated etc. As far as he was concerned, it was a pain in the arse.

For me, that was an opportunity and I had a look, here was someone with a problem that needed solving. The screen system was supported by a slotted aluminium frame that was as solid as a rock. If I could build a structure around the screens that was tied into the frame and not attached to walls or bolted to the floor and made from metal, we could be onto something.

That evening I investigated aluminium frames. I knew a bit about extrusion because I was a rep for a company a few years before. I obtained a sample I thought would work and took it to the control room where it connected perfectly. The next step was to work out what it would cost. So after a few sketches to some specialists and some internet research, I arrived at a cost to me of around £300. I thought I would charge £400 for the parts making a 25% mark-up, then charge £200 for my time as I thought that it would take a day to do. I talked my mate into giving me a go and my first ever order was received for £600, brilliant, I was in business.

That is how my business started. I purchased aluminium extrusion from the internet and I cut them to size in my dad's garage to form simple adjustable frames. The most important thing was that it worked and it solved the customer's problem – one that he was willing to pay to be resolved. What I had done was found out how to make something that somebody wanted.

This was the point Michael was trying to make during that question and answer session. Your idea does not have to be unique, of course, it would be great if it was, but that is not vital to have a successful product. You need to provide a product or service that people want. You do not necessarily need a lot of people to want it. Having a niche product is OK, and in some cases, it is an advantage because it can remove some competition. For example, major mass market companies, who focus on volume, probably will not be interested, but it is important to know who they are. Most people who start a company are not amazing original ideas people. Entrepreneurs are classic non detail, extroverted, calculated risk takers and not necessarily intellects, scientists or IT specialists. My business was not some crazy brainwave at all. I took an aluminium frame system, which was completely known technology, and used it to solve a customer's problem. I then bolted other products to it and, eventually, I bolted other businesses to it. Every day since, I have looked for customers with problems, who are prepared to pay me to fix them.

If you can come up with something that people want that they did not realise they wanted, then that is even more amazing. The best example I can give you is the camera on your phone and texting! Think about the 1980s when mobile phones were new. The technology was so fast moving before we knew it. We were using phones to text and then to take photographs. It makes perfect sense now, people are sending more text messages in various formats and taking and sending more photos than ever. Who would have thought of it? Someone worked out that we would rather send a written note than talk in person! Or is that more of a journey where we have evolved into a society that now feels uncomfortable to call and speak to someone?

Hats off to companies like Apple and several others to have built up a reputation of development in solving problems that we do not know we have! This is highlighted by pre-sales of the latest Apple phones before they are launched, and before people even know what they can do, they have already decided they will upgrade. This is as much marketing, fashion, and reputation as it is technology.

This book is not about Apple or other famous brands. It is about everyday small start-ups and how you can scale back these big solutions. Let me give you another example of something that really worked on a much smaller scale.

A friend of mine runs a great pizza takeaway on the outskirts of Winchester. He set this up in a place where there were already two pizza takeaways and lots of other fast-food establishments. So how did it work? He simply did his homework. He found out that a new housing estate was being built and the prices of the property were eye watering. He looked at the competition and realised there was an opportunity for a much high-end handmade product, in-house made dough with high-end toppings that wealthier people would pay for. So was there a problem that needed solving in that these new customers could get budget pizza but not high-quality Pizza? Possibly not, but then, perhaps, he showed customers locally that they actually had a distinct choice. He also built a reputation. It was a cool thing to have his van outside your home! It showed you wanted a better product and were prepared to pay a little more for it. Would this solution work in a less affluent area, possibly not!

When you see these massive chain stores appear, be aware of where they are, because I can guarantee that a great deal of work has gone into selecting their locations. Higher end stores like M&S and Waitrose need a certain type of customer, makes perfect sense really.

Of course, it is not all about location, but that is not the point here. Know who your customers are and where they are. Work out how to get what you have in front of them. Work out how to demonstrate how you can fix their problem. Do your homework before you start anything else because to get here might be impossible if you start somewhere other than there!

Chapter Two
Where the Hell are We Going?

How can you tell you have arrived, if you do not know what the destination looks like?

OK, so I am not a details person and apparently, that is a classic entrepreneur's trait. Not a great one but, hey, in my case, it is true. Realising what you are is both good and bad. It is vital to learn and understand. We will go into that in some detail later but knowing your skills and limits can only be good. The normal way to find out what you are good at is to have a go and never worry about failing. This will just tell you what you are not so good at. Learn from it and have another go but, perhaps, in a different way. Knowing you have weaknesses is liberating and living with them makes you a better person. Sometimes in business, perhaps, we do need to hide business weakness but, hey, most companies exaggerate the good things as well.

This chapter is about planning and why it is so important. A study in the USA showed that students, who had a plan after graduation, were more successful than the ones who did not. In business, this is the same. People who have written a plan are much more likely to be successful than those that have not, even if the plan they have written is not followed. I ended up with plan C which was fine, it is your plan, so you can change it as many times as you like.

My first plan more or less went completely tits up from day one. Chapter one tells you to find a solution to someone's problem, provide something somebody wants or, perhaps, 'take away someone's pain' as it was described to me once.

Before I even started, there was a problem. I needed a business bank account. I needed to be tax registered and I needed some sort of insurance. My first job, as mentioned in chapter one, was not great. It required two trips to site because I had not noticed that the floor and walls were all pissed and not straight. This required an additional £100 in more materials. I forgot to add in the fuel or the business car insurance premium I needed! Yes, not so much as no plan, more like no clue! If I had, perhaps, spent slightly longer considering a plan of action, it could have gone better. So I made a few mistakes and that was OK. I knew I was going to make mistakes but at least I was making something!

I learnt a lot from this first job. I was determined to make sure the job was perfect when I finished it and it was. That was important to me in building a relationship with my client because I knew that he would remember me for the goods and services I provided. It was important he was happy with the end result, even though I had made additional visits to get it right.

A few weeks later, the sales guy for the rear projector screens called me and asked to meet. He wanted to use me to offer the cladding as a service to future projects. I agreed on the understanding that he also gave me a list of the jobs he had already done, so I could expand my client base and offer them this new solution.

It was not an endless list, so I knew it was not going to be a career move, however, it did give me the opportunity to learn more and get involved with control rooms. I had a history working in control rooms but that was many years ago, so to get up-to-date information was going to be key if I was going to generate a business in that area. I chatted to several end users and other companies in the industry and discovered the market for control rooms was big, very big.

I arranged a visit with someone I knew based in a London control room. He was an East-End guy, a straight talker with many years of experience running a big CCTV control room managing cameras looking at both the road network and public spaces. We got chatting and he was talking about how fast the technology was changing and how it was a struggle to keep in touch with the latest developments but that his main problem was how some of his providers were simply not keeping up with things. He showed me a case in point when we walked into another room, there was a wooden control console, hand crafted to house lots of screens and other technology. He told me it was a year old and was going in the skip because all the technology had changed and the mountings, openings and ergonomics were now different. My eyes lit up, could I solve this problem for him and how much would he pay me to fix this? He told me what he paid for the console, how long it had lasted and why it was no longer suitable. It was at this moment that I saw the opportunity to build and supply custom made furniture.

I used the extrusion I had purchased on the internet along with plastic panels from a wholesaler, who also gave me the details of a company who could cut them to size. I then trolled the web for all the other accessories needed. I talked to a local carpentry company who manufactured a worktop for me and within a month I had my first console that had the capability of being changed and adjusted as the technology it housed changed. The prototype had been built using notebook sketches. I knew this was not the way forward so had to find someone who could use Computer Aided Design (CAD) as it was beyond my capability. (I still cannot use CAD today). When it was finished, it was definitely not pretty, some would say ugly but I would suggest it was utilitarian! It did not make me any money, which was a worry but what it did do was give me enough information to see the potential because is basically worked and solved the customers problem. A new plan was needed.

I decided to start writing in detail what I was going to need to start manufacturing consoles. The list got longer and longer because at that moment I did not know where to begin but the world wide web came to my rescue. Three months later I am in a barn with a bench, chop saw, table saw a pillar drill and internet access. I then had to design a range of extrusions and connectors to actually build something! I also needed to find a reliable CAD designer to complete the drawings for me.

I had met a guy previously when working at another company, who had just started to do some freelance CAD design, so I used him to draw up some extrusion. I never forget him saying to me, 'What are they?', when he handed me the designs, I simply said thanks, paid him and told him they would pay off my mortgage one day! What I did not realise is they would also pay off his mortgage as within six months he became my operations director and is still with me today 18 years later.

My plan started getting some detail. I talked to friends and people I knew to get advice. I had no clue about business finance but needed to learn. Luckily, I had a couple of friends who were accountants and they were invaluable in helping me get started. Never forget to talk to your friends as you just never know who they know. It sounds a bit daft but friendship is so important to me and I work very hard to keep in contact with people. It is so easy nowadays with various messaging apps. A quick 'how are you' is so easy and can mean such a lot. When you get more corporate, this is called networking!

I cannot tell you how important a plan is, that is what this chapter is about. I knew I wanted to take over the world and not just be a one-man band. That made me register the company as 'Limited' from the start. It also meant I was going to try and be an employer so needed to get the correct accountancy software in from the start. I knew I wanted my own product, so I wrote a plan to develop the product and keep it unique. This does not have to be massively detailed. My first plan was five pages and now the company business plan (that is reviewed every year) is still only about a dozen pages long.

I kept talking to people, building relationships, listening, and learning. The rep who gave me some business from the rear projector screen company is still a friend over 15 years later. We are still in contact today.

Have a plan for yourself as well. How big do you want to be? When are you going to stop? If your business plan is to only employ one person and just stay small, then that is great. It is your plan, do not beat yourself up if the plan goes tits up. Just write another plan and start again. Nobody has gone through life without making a mistake here or there. Remember, it is common for people getting to the end of their lives to regret the things they didn't do rather than the things they did.

Write a plan, after all you cannot get where you are going without some idea of the route.

Chapter Three
Bread and Butter

I started my business with every penny I had and every penny I could borrow. The method I used to borrow is a confession story. I will give you that later in this chapter, but the 'Bread and Butter' comes from something my mum told me. She said to focus on the bread and butter and every now and again taste some jam. She was talking about looking after your family by providing the basics first, forgetting vanity and not being distracted. A distraction can take many formats, but think of this as, perhaps, being side-tracked into things that you might like doing but, that does not actually give you the day-to-day money you need. Bread and butter is basically money. It is the money to feed yourself and pay your mortgage. Mum and Dad were the most non-materialistic people I knew. They loved the simple things and a holiday once a year was the exception, not the norm until their later years.

If you are truly driven like most entrepreneurs are, then the chances are you want more, a lot more. In truth, you will probably want more until you die and I am not talking work now. Finding contentment and being satisfied for me is the challenge and apparently, that is common in business owners. This is covered later, but it can be a real issue for highly motivated people. They often crave more success. This can make achieving contentment difficult and may, perhaps, lead them to becoming a workaholic. Remember, a workaholic finds it hard to trust people to get a job done. They tend to be control freaks, which in turn leads to a larger workload. This can lead to illness and can affect your personal life.

When it comes to business, I used Mum's analogy and twisted it to its more basic saying of bread meaning money. You must look after your money and more to the point remember that 'Cash is King'. This is all about cash flow. Without positive cash flow, you could fold before you get going. I nearly did.

Cash flow is a business term that simply means you need to manage money in such a way that you always have some. If you use overdrafts or loans, these can count, but must be included in the cash flow forecast as part of your plan. OK, another thing to explain.

Here is an example: If you sell bread (see what I did there), you have to buy the ingredients, make the dough, wait for it to rise, bake the bread, package the bread and then sell it. Every part of this process in a business costs money. Purchasing ingredients or materials, investing in labour to make the dough, financing the time of raising the dough (perhaps heating and lighting), then the fuel to bake the bread, then the packaging and selling of the product. When you get paid, the banking costs need to be paid and then the government will want some of the money by way of taxes (never ever forget this bit). All of this requires an investment in time and money that you are spending or lending the business until you sell the bread and get paid for it. Of course, the plan is that your investment means the bread is wonderful and worth a lot more. This increases the value to the customer (you can now charge more) and you make a nice profit. You then repeat the process.

But how much bread are you going to sell? This is the question. Notice, the question was not how many ingredients can you afford? That would lead us into talking about supply and demand, market research, who is going to buy your bread and where you will sell it. At the moment, I just want to talk about cash flow. If you have lots of people wanting bread, you could run out of money before you deliver the bread and get paid.

It is quite simple to write a timeline of the risk and exposure of your cash flow to begin with. As you go through the bread making process, the investment rises (see what I did again!) with the time and effort you put in. If you sell all the bread on one day, in one place, with any luck, all the money comes back and bang, you have your butter!

You can then plan the next cycle of production remembering to base it on the experience of the last one. Big tip here. Keep learning and keep listening to your customers as demand is constantly changing. It is what we are always trying to improve. You might need to change the recipe or perhaps how you market it if your customer's tastes change or different products have a greater demand.

It gets more complicated as you grow, your bills for the investment come in at different times and your staff will want to be paid monthly and not when the bread is sold. The tax man definitely knows when he wants to get paid. As your empire grows, things can get better or worse and are sometimes out of your control all together.

Thinking Space (my first business) has gone through two tough periods. The first was a recession in 2008. We had people, a workshop, and materials, but nobody was buying. The business had to cut staff quickly because reducing fixed costs quickly i.e. building and insurance fees etc. was impossible.

Our second bad spell included a bad debt. A bad debt is a fancy way of saying a company does not pay you and they then go out of business before you can get anything back. I have seen the collapse of some firms take down lots of sub suppliers. There are various tools in place to protect you but in the early days, you just need to push as hard as you can for payment before delivery. I still do that now, if I can. We now run with a bad debt provision, that is to say ,we allow some money in our forecasting for the year to cover someone who does not pay us.

The best model for cash flow would be to pay your suppliers when you get paid yourself. It is not easy, but is possible and the most famous people, who do this, are the big supermarket chains. They often go to providers and negotiate long payment terms, but expect the shopper to pay at the time of purchase. Not a surprise that this cash rich model gives the supermarkets the ability to use the cash to get into new sectors of business that require good finance such as insurance, currency exchange and banking! Now be very careful of when you sign contracts with people who put this in a clause leaving you with the shit end of the stick. Often, you end up with no control of when you get paid. My top tip here is to watch the big blue-chip companies. They are usually the ones who use your desire to work with them as a well-known company to their advantage.

Now, the confession I promised regarding borrowing:

When I first started my company, I put in every penny I had. I sold a motorbike, an old car and moved to my parents to save money. I also went to the bank for a loan and back in 2003, every bank I went to wanted guarantees. I did try my bank first, only to be told they did not do business banking! School boy error on my part because they were actually a building society! I tried several other banks but they all wanted me to offer my home as security which was not possible as I was going through a divorce and I was reasonably positive asking my ex-wife if I could secure a loan on the house she was living in was not going to fly! It meant I had to get money another way. A few years earlier, I did have a small personal loan to buy a car and knew the process. I was still in the final throws of my employee wage slips that had come from the job I left to start my business which meant on paper I looked like a safe person to lend money to. I have to say right now that this is strictly 'a little bit illegal' because I am sure you have to say you have a job (that I did) and that it paid you enough money to pay back the loan.

So, I returned to my bank and asked to talk about a personal loan for a car! I remember this young lady saying to me, "Sure, this is very straight forward." (Remember, I have been to every high street bank trying to borrow money for the new business and now, apparently, to lend me money is 'straight forward'.) "And we can give you a decision right away." She asked me how much I wanted and I replied simply with "how much can I have?" (I got that line from my kids). She looked me up and down and said,

"Sorry, sir, it does not work like that." So, I thought for a bit and said,

"£20,000, please." She sat at her computer, typed away, then looked over her glasses at me and said under her breath, "Um, try £17,000." I did, and within 15 minutes, I was off spending my personal loan of 17 grand on saws and aluminium extrusion.

This amount of bread was what I needed to get the butter I wanted! I was off and running. I would add that I paid off the loan many years ago and never missed a payment during its term.

Chapter Four
Don't Know It, Buy It

This chapter could also be called 'Don't try to learn something new right now', it also relates to your own personal focus. I would say the selected title does roll better.

When I started off, there were just loads of things that needed to be done that required different skill sets. In the modern world, you can find a lot on the internet to help with the basics and I will touch on this later. With so many things to do, it is vital that you recognise what you are good at, what you can manage and, what you really have no bloody clue about! I would suggest it is as important to recognise where you are weak as much as knowing what you are good at.

When I started Thinking Space, from day one, I had no idea about accounting and tax returns. It was clear I would need some expert advice, not only to set things up correctly, but to look at what I needed to do regularly and how to manage it. I had a good friend, Graham Taylor, who was a partner in an accountancy firm, so I approached him to see if he could help. Like a lot of business owners, I learn from people who have done it rather than people who have only written about it. That sounds like a dig at the teaching sector, but it is not at all. What I would say is in the training and teaching world, you do not experience the business pressures and that pressure changes your approach. I had several conversations with Graham over a pint or two, and at the end of our meetings, he did me a great favour and turned me down in regard to being my accountant! He explained that his company had, and still has a very good corporate reputation, and could offer all the services I would ever need. They were a medium sized, local firm, with several regional offices, but they were simply too big for me at the start. I did not need investment advice and I was not interested in technical tax expertise for international trade at that time. What I needed was a small local office of accountants that specialised in companies of my size.

I suspect the real reason for not taking my business was that he could not make enough money out of me, but I do respect him for letting me down gently and not telling me directly that my business in a dining room was just too small! It was only five years later, that his company became our accountants and believe me, over the last ten years or so, he has made plenty of money from us and still is!

I did some research and found a small, but professional firm, a local high street accountant that was working with new businesses and had some experience with manufacturing companies. Without realising it, I had written a mini requirement document, a wish list of minimum needs I had, and things I needed to learn. At that time, it was important to be able to ring them to get support and advice without getting an invoice every time I called. They gave me a simple spread sheet to work with, which I actually used for many years. It was easy to keep updated. I did not have to spend too much time on it or think too much about accounting until we met each quarter for a coffee and catch up. What I had done was learnt the basics and delegated the rest, including the tax returns, so I could crack on with other functions within the business. In addition, it also gave me another advisor, another contact and another person to learn from.

At that time, I also purchased a cheap CRM (customer relationship management) database. It was £100 and it gave me the ability to build my customer contact list in a way that was organised. I simply picked the software because I knew it. It was not the best and was definitely out of date when I compared it with some of the amazing systems which were out there but it simply meant I did not have another thing to learn. I purchased it on the approval of my accountant, who said simply that I had enough to do, and learning a new system was not going to reduce my workload. He was completely right. I would recommend a CRM system as one of your early investments, it kept me focused on sales. Every day, I would log in to see who I needed to talk to and I would update it after each call. All basic stuff, but I chased every quotation and every invoice using that system. Nowadays, you can probably get something free online but if you do, then make sure you keep the data backed up and in date.

Getting technical and expert advice and support is even more important now. I see issues in the business every day when we should, perhaps, bring in an expert and not do things ourselves. Because we are now larger, the challenge is that the requirements get more detailed, so it is not often we can just ring somebody. Now we need to create a plan, a requirement and a scope of work along with a budget. Often we want three quotes, so need to write a specification. Of course, this is all useful and the right way to do things but always remember that the point is to solve a problem, save money and time, fill a skills gap or have something provided we are not great at or simply cannot do. If the value to the business is small, you must have to have the ability to bypass all the processes. Only recently within my business I found a colleague going through a lengthy tendering process for a piece of machinery that had a value of only £1,500. The work involved would outweigh the value of any saving we would make on getting the best deal. It was probably more important to select the correct machine and just get on with it!

This scenario is common within big companies, where the process dictates that a ten-page document needs to be completed and signed off by two or three people in order to get something done, even if it is small and simple to do. Be aware of being too bureaucratic.

So, the 'buy it' idea all sounds like common sense but when you do not have any money because you have only just started your business, you do have to do a lot yourself and simply put the hours in.

I mentioned the World Wide Web earlier as a resource. The internet is a wonderful resource for helping companies start up. In a world of openness, there seems to be an endless supply of downloads providing help and information. My only advice here is to take your time selecting what you need. The internet has a lot of American influence and try to ensure you do not break any copywrite rules.

With good research (not selecting information from the first three pages of any search engine, perhaps), you can get lots of documentation for free or for a small fee. I remember dropping my company logo on lots of documents, everything from terms and conditions, job application forms for staff, quotation templates, HR documents and various company policies.

Just remember, doing this type of work will not sell a product, raise your brand or introduce you to a customer, so stay focused. I know a lot of companies who have gone to the wall despite having a large employee handbook, a company car policy, a holiday booking system and a company logo. What they did not have was orders! I have seen very hi-tech companies fail. They have an amazing product, but nobody who would buy it knows about it because they do not have a commercial person promoting it. It is so easy to set up a company and have everything you need in place except any actual business. Please, be aware of working hard on the wrong thing! It is fun doing things you like to do and are good at but they might not be the things you NEED to do to win business! It is not so easy to ring a potential client scouting for work or asking someone for an order. If you are not the person to do that leg work, that is OK, but if you do not know how to do it, 'buy it'.

When I started Thinking Space, I wanted 'world domination'. Now that sounds like a proper wonky thing to say but it says we want to grow as a global player. We want employees and we want employees in different countries. We want to be a major player and have a good reputation in our line of business. Before you even start looking at getting skills in, you must think about what you need now and what you will need tomorrow as they will not be the same. This is difficult as some things will grow with you but not everything or everyone. The people who were with you at the start of the business may no longer be the right people when the company is 40 people strong.

The plan could be for world domination or as a sole trader working locally. To achieve both of these might possibly include skills that you do not have. These are the things that you need to buy in.

Chapter Five
Work the Numbers

Working the numbers came in as an expression when I recruited my first sales guy. In fact, that sales guy is now a partner and the current commercial director. We still work the numbers today. This is how I have been operating for many years and it has really worked for me. Not only does it measure your performance in different areas but it keeps you focused on the things that will grow the business, especially in the early days when there are so many things to do.

When Paul started, his number one job was to grow sales. Sounds easy and it is something that every company that has a desire to grow wants to do, of course. We worked on a plan of daily tasks and habits, that if you do them every day and every week lead to a growth in sales. The key was to make this his sole aim, day in and day out. If the habits and tasks were good, the sales would improve and others within the business would handle everything else.

The idea is simple, so think of it like this. If you focus on results, you might never change but if you focus on change, you should get results.

Now there is some bad news. In the early days of the business, the most efficient method I found to grow the business was to call people. Get on the phone and speak to them. The focus should not be on social media or attending network events. You need to simply get on the phone and find someone that uses/could use/will know someone who could use or has a requirement for the product or service you provide. I call this the bad news because generally people do not like doing this, other jobs are easier and many find it difficult calling a stranger. It is much easier to tweet or Facebook your product as you can do this sat at home in front of the TV. For me, in the early days, the most efficient and effective way was to do the really hard task of cold calling.

So, what has this got to do with 'working the numbers'? Simple, it is a tough job that you will avoid, so you set up a challenge of numbers. Every single day for the first three years of Thinking Space, I made calls until I got the contact details of one person who had not heard of us before but had or may have a requirement for a custom made console. That was easy then, but even now, there are people in my industry that still do not know who we are and what we do. I then started to build a database, adding only key contacts so that I knew who I needed to talk to next time and recording information that would help me to start building a relationship. It was time consuming to get the name of a CCTV control room manager or the head of engineering at an airport but once you achieved that it was an amazing feeling. In this instance, working the numbers was one a day, so once this was achieved, you could then get on with the fun stuff the rest of the day.

Working the numbers, it's not just a tool to use when you first start up. Once my business started to grow, I looked at our call history and worked out that for every ten people I contacted, one of them had a live project. When Paul joined, having two of us on the phones meant we were quoting one project a week. We started to see a trend. We were winning around one in three projects quoted. Actually, to start with it was higher, perhaps, one out of 2.2 jobs quoted, but we had low overheads in the barn so our price was more competitive. This data was like striking gold. It gave us knowledge for production. When the quote numbers increased, we knew to get stock in and to let production know that we were going to be busy as the orders would follow.

We would also set a task in our database to send a mail shot to all our perspective clients once a month and then once every two months, each one got a call. As the database grew, this meant that we knew which clients needed to be called each day. Another numbers game and this was in addition to the cold calling we had already tasked ourselves with.

We then started to attend networking events. I set myself an objective of attending once a month. I also read a lot of management books as part of my own education and development and tasked myself to read two chapters a week.

As we grew, I set a challenge of trying to output £100,000 per person. That meant with me, my partners, Paul Roberts and Paul Atkins, and a fitter we were trying to manufacture £400k in a year. Working back from this 'target' of £400k, we could calculate our budgeting and forecast both profit and what room we had left for investment and growth.

The next question we started to discuss was, what is important about the win rate? I still use the win rate as a benchmark for our selling price today in some sectors. It is quite broad brush but it is a nice little indicator, although it will not work everywhere. As a general rule, our decision and set up was that if we won one project in three, our bid and pricing was about right for the market. If we were winning more than one in three bids, I would ease the price up and charge a little more increasing the margin. If we were winning less, I would check we were going after the right work. Note, I did not drop the price, I never wanted to be the cheapest. My mission was to be the best and that required investment, which I could only do if we made a profit.

We also use numbers to help manage time. If a project is going to take a couple of months, we break it down into chunks. It is a question of 'How do you eat an elephant?', "One bite at a time!" Simply put, break a big project down and set small goals or milestones. Every day, spend an hour on it, a morning or one day a week. Later, we got into SMART working. There are lots of books on this, so will not go into this in detail but every task needs to be specific, measurable, achievable, relevant and time bound. It has been around for years and it works.

You can have some fun with this and it keeps things moving in the office. Every time we achieved something important that week, we went to the pub on the Friday after work for a pint to celebrate. Interestingly, I did not realise until later how important this was. It cemented our relationship and made the three directors friends and reminded us we were doing OK.

It is quite a process working the numbers and I can see that this would not work for everybody. For me, it was a constant reminder of what really needed to be done and not perhaps what I wanted to actually do as I have mentioned previously these are often not the same thing sadly.

As a business owner, you report to nobody, so you need self-discipline and the ability to self-start every single day. No one is going to tell you off and no one will fire you but to set an example to colleagues and to have done this leg work means that a lazy salesperson or employee cannot take you for a ride.

Working out what the numbers represent and which ones are the priority is the next challenge. If you feel writing a blog every day will grow, what you do the fastest then crack on but if you do that for a month and it does not produce the response you need, then try something else. Only madmen (and mostly football managers) will keep doing the same thing all the time expecting the result to change!

What has been interesting within our business is how this process has nearly been reversed now that the company is larger. Each year, we start budgeting for the next financial year and it starts with the agreed sales target. Our commercial director reports on where he sees growth and what that looks like in regard to product sales by sector. He estimates this by using the historical information he has and by the performance of his numbers running up to the year end. In addition to that, he includes in some known and unknown factors. An unknown factor is not part of the numbers game but something that he expects to affect his performance in either a positive or negative way. Let me give you a few examples.

A looming recession or global pandemic! These are going to possibly have a negative effect. What is interesting regarding budgeting is that the existing order book could also be effected? For us, it was a case of our fitters not being allowed on site to complete installations. Government and national changes or regulation can either be negative or positive on your business depending on what you do. If your paint product is banned because it is not fire retardant, then it is bad but if a competitor's product is legislated against, then it is good! If a competitor is taken over or closes, this could have an effect on you. These are all things you cannot control but perhaps they are things you can plan for.

Investment in new people is great but it can take a little while before you see the reward of this investment and so this can be a factor. In addition, you will find that any new products, marketing launches or changes to market sectors will all influence the business.

Once you have the headline numbers for your budget, we then, of course, challenge them and push the commercial department to increase them. Once the haggling is completed, we feed this back into a very simple accounts spreadsheet. We identify what we want our profit margin to be and then carve up the rest of the budgeted income. The material costs are calculated proportional to sales as well as direct labour costs, all of which are aimed around the gross profit percentage. Then you have the indirect costs that affect the net profit such as marketing, IT and admin just to name a few. The result is really simple as you can see what you need to output in a year to be able to make the margins and achieve the budgets you set. Remember, this is your forecast and you can change and alter it during the year. It is a great tool to keep control of the numbers.

Once the budget is worked out, we make sure that every number has someone in the management team accountable for it; marketing, stationary, insurance, vehicle maintenance, rent, rates, travel expenses etc., every penny is the responsibility of someone and their job is to achieve best value. Note, I did not say reduce it. If we need more people because we are busy, then the budget is going to increase. That is fine because if we do it correctly, the profit increases at the same time. We do, however, need to ensure we get the right people for the right money.

Just as a foot note and something to consider. During a downturn, it is common for businesses to cut the same two areas. These are generally IT investment and marketing because they are the easiest things you can instantly stop. Only you can decide which areas of your business should be cut back to ensure you survive.

Chapter Six
Jam Tomorrow

This expression came from my mum and I love it. I can only assume it is an old expression.

I started Thinking Space in my mum and dad's dining room, then I moved into a barn and things grew from there. In the first year I would work half at home at the dining table and the rest of the time I would be at the barn.

For the first 18 months, I think, I was doing a minimum of a 12-hour day for six days a week and I never ever switched off. Some weeks I would work through the weekend and my stress level would rise as the money got tighter or things did not go my way. At the time I was lucky to have an accommodating girlfriend and two wonderful parents that let me live rent free for nearly a year.

The first few projects I completed were made using extrusion purchased online, which I cut to length and some ready machined panels purchased locally. I would then hire a van and build on site to fit the control room. Because I was only adding a small amount of value to the solution, the margin was tight. I remember getting back from South Wales and sending an invoice to the customer the following morning while having a cup of tea with Mum. I was cheeky and on the invoice I included an additional fee because of the Severn Bridge toll.

She was proud that I was making a go of it (although she never actually said that to my face, of course) and asked where I had been the day before. I laughed when she said I was now an international businessman because I worked in Wales! However, I was not in a good place. With the invoice sent, I worked out that the job had probably made me £50 for two days work. It was not much and that is when Mum told me the 'jam tomorrow' line. She said to me that right now I had to look after the bread and butter because the jam will come tomorrow!

For me, one thing that you cannot really do in the early days is something for nothing or a 'loss leader' as it is sometimes put. This is a project that you do for no money or a loss because it will lead to bigger things. It is fine if you have the money to invest or lose and you have a plan and strategy on how the investment is going to pay back but not something you can do as a start-up because of the planning you need and the exposure you want to produce from it. It is easy to be talked into this and often an over keen salesperson will tell you all about the business tomorrow. Be brave and value what you are offering. Jam tomorrow is acceptable but make sure the bread and butter is so good and thick that it looks a bit like jam today!

I always measure sales performance in a number of ways. To avoid rewarding a person, who is giving away margin, make sure it is in the bonus calculations. I know some companies do not like to tell staff about the margins made but you can still manage the margins. If salespeople have spread sheets and discount structures, then they know their boundaries without the need for detailed profit information. Think of it like this. If you were a salesperson and you had 20 Porsche cars to sell next month but were given no other objectives, just remember that anyone can sell a new Porsche for £100, hey, presto, your salesperson has hit target.

Not everyone will have the same ethical barometer as you. There are some countries or more specifically, nationalities that will simply lie and promise you the earth and not deliver. Any loss in margin might not be down to your sales team, so make sure you know the facts (know the numbers). Do not get hung up on this because the work ethic changes around the world and the cultures and approach to business vary by region. It is nothing personal. There are some things we probably cannot control but just being aware of cultural differences within the sales function does give you an edge.

Now our business is established, we do complete the odd small project as a sample or vastly discounted but it is completely managed and budgeted for. When you start to manage a sales team, you will soon see which of them 'give' the product away. Some seem to demand sample after sample to go their clients but remember, this could be the market sector or geographic area they cover. Just be wary and manage the costs and expectations of both the sales team and their customers.

After sending the invoice to Wales, I called the user to check he was happy with the work. He was over the moon and had another couple of sites for me to quote. While on the phone, I had to let him know that I made nothing on the job and that the next project would see an uplift. His response was great. He said he was surprised at the price I did it for and thought I had got it wrong. While we were talking, I used the opportunity to calculate the 'real' price it should have been and what I would change moving forward which I then discussed with him. I wanted to make sure it would not come as a shock the next time and wanted to be straight with him.

He did not bat an eyelid and said, "Stick to the truth, Wayne." A positive outcome for both of us. I could not have afforded to work for him otherwise. For around three years after that, he was my most regular client. I learnt a lot from the experience. You have to try to speak the truth even when the conversation can be difficult.

Always think about the value you and your business add to a solution. We are all trying to solve a problem or take the pain away from someone in a way. As a modern business, we now have to compete with the internet. We embrace that challenge. Not only do we sell products via our site and portals but through the traditional channels of exhibitions, events and old-fashioned sales rep's. All of these things have value. Try to remember the value you add to a product.

I have a situation going on currently where I am purchasing a small business that includes a spares department. During some early checking of the numbers, I noticed two things. The first one was the employee managing spares was knowledgeable and very good with customers. Nothing was too much trouble and often he would spend 30 minutes on the phone helping a customer out. The trouble was he did not value this advice. When the same customer then quoted internet prices, he would fold and drop his price to match it. He had forgotten the value he added. He had not considered how much his advice and expertise was worth and the fact that he was spending more time providing 'free' advice rather than selling spares. How do you change this approach? There are a few methods that can be adopted but this is how we worked on changing the 'free advice' approach.

The first is to value time and avoid helping the person on the phone right away. We want the customer to value his/her time. To do this, we simply state you are working on another job and cannot talk but you can agree to arrange a 15-minute call later. The idea is not to put them off completely but to make them aware that your time is important. The 15-minute chat is free and quick. Find out what the issue is and what they have done so far? This question gives you the opportunity to assess how much effort they have put into this so far and are not just calling because they are driving and have time to kill. If they push for a solution or detail, then push back and simply state you cannot help without more detailed assessment and that a survey maybe required which costs time and money.

People will pay for good service, believe me and that is why the internet sales market will not complete destroy the high street. Things in retail will really change over the next five years as they have already done but good service and support will always be valuable. We want our pain taken away and our problem solved as consumers.

The 'Jam Tomorrow' title also links to 'Cash is King' as well as a number of other areas. You have to be careful who you give credit to because you will never get to eat jam unless you get paid. In addition to this, knowing what your business is good at and most profitable at, will get you to jam faster. I will cover that in detail later.

More than 18 years later, I know how nice jam tastes and it is better than bread alone!

Chapter Seven
Bush Tucker Trial

This is one of the most important chapters to understand, however, it is not as easy to do as the explanation. I am sure you have heard of a 'Bush Tucker Trial', in which you go through a series of meals, eating something more and more disgusting each time until the final thing you must eat to complete the task is completely terrible. The reward is not earned until you have managed to overcome the final obstacle. What if you ate the worst most disgusting thing first? Then the other items would not be as bad, would they?

You are probably wondering how this equates to business? Well, imagine you have a 'to do list' with 30 tasks. If on your list is something that you really do not like doing or are not good at (the final plate of food), the chances are you will never get to it because you will continue to put other items in front of it. Now you might consider that a result after all you might have knocked 25 other jobs off your list, so you will be feeling good. However, what you have done is prioritised the work you have to do by how you feel and, perhaps, how easy the tasks are. What you need to do is prioritise in an order that shows what really needs to be done and is most important to the business.

When I write a daily 'to do list', I run down the tasks and give them a score of one, two or three with one being something that needs to be done right away and number three a lower priority. When I started the business, nearly all my items were a number one and they all seemed sales based. I always had a re-occurring item that was a number one and that was to call someone I had not spoken to before, who could be a potential customer. I mentioned this in the 'numbers game' chapter.

It is easy to have a list of 30/40 tasks that include calling a few suppliers, buying samples and stock and generally spending a little money. It is not so easy to do the difficult jobs because they usually take time and perhaps three or four sessions before they are completed. I suggest that every day you eat (complete) the biggest challenge first. I never enjoyed calling people who had never heard of me and it took forever to eventually get past the receptionist to the buyer or security manager or air traffic control engineer, who could possibly have a requirement. But what I did know was that if I was going to sell more product, I needed these people to know me and my business. Once I got their details, I then went onto number two on my list to follow up/say hello to ten existing contacts.

I read a book a few years ago called *Eat that Frog* by Brian Tracy and it is one I suggest you read as it is sort of what this chapter is about. In simple terms, what he suggests is that if the worst thing you have to do is eat a frog, then get on with it because the rest of the day is clear and you will not have the frog looking at you all day!

The next question is how you select which jobs are a number one, two or three. The good thing is that it is completely up to you, after all you are the boss. If you pick wisely, then often it will be a key factor in both the speed of growth of your business and your efficiency.

A good suggestion when prioritising is working to get a balance. I have seen some managers divide up their day into time zones. For example, three hours in sales, three in production and three in admin. It is about discipline and if that works for you, then go for it. My concern with this method might be that it is a little too rigid.

You will find as you employ more people that one of your key functions will be to set objectives and goals, which are just ways in which you ensure your team also do the right stuff first and not the easy stuff. Your role in a way is getting them to select the 'number one' tasks first and not the easier 'number threes'. Getting your team to focus on the correct priorities of the business is a real challenge. I have seen a lot of busy companies go under because they are not focused correctly and sometimes when you are looking in from the outside, it is so obvious.

This subject can be taken further because we can start talking about time management and as the business grows, you can employ people to complete the more important tasks first, again speeding up efficiency and then growth.

When I started out on my own, I knew the key was to get orders and win business. I needed to get my name out there but, more importantly, I needed to get in front of the right people and not just randomly approach things because my product was so niche.

I have made lots of mistakes but one thing I learnt fast was where I had to focus my time. I spent way too long at networking events with other start-up businesses. A networking day is easy, a few biscuits and a few cups of coffee is an easy way to meet people but for me, not the right way. I needed to talk to people who were in the market for consoles. These people were not local or attending small events. They were at global exhibitions, so that was where I needed to be.

The Bush Tucker evidence presents itself clearly if we you do not define a person's role and responsibilities. You will find gaps forming around tasks that need to be completed but have been left. This was evident when I purchased a mature but small business, problems were caused by a lack of clear priorities. The team were young and although they were busy and hardworking, they spent their days 'firefighting' and dealing with work as it came in, picking and choosing what they did first, without following a clear process to log the work and prioritise. Can you imagine the challenge here if the work that was needed to be done was customer focused? The damage to the reputation of the business could have had a long tern effect.

The good news is that this can be rectified by clear objective setting, management and if required, training, to make the bush tucker trial less of a challenge or onerous task for the person responsible.

Chapter Eight
Who Dares Win?

No surprise about what we are going to talk about here: RISK!

The day you even consider starting a business on your own, you are taking a risk. Even in the early days, if it is only about the investment in time you are losing something, you will never get back. I definitely missed around three years of my children growing up because I only saw them really for a few hours a couple of days a week.

The amount of risk you are prepared to take includes several areas including money, reputation and time. This has to be balanced with your attitude to risk. I cannot highlight enough that being an entrepreneur is not for everyone. Some people cope with levels of stress better and some start-ups need a bigger risk exposure to get them going than others. I am a firm believer that some levels of stress help you focus and up your game. I played football for many years and always remember wanting to play in the bigger more important games. The standards of everyone involved including mine would go up and the natural focus would be sharper. Having said that, there are limits to levels of stress exposure and this is something you must work out for yourself.

As we know, even banks are aware of this. Remember when I started Thinking Space, I could not get a business loan because the banks would only really match what I was prepared to risk financially (fair enough) and at that time I did not have anything to risk! Once the company was profitable, then all sorts of lenders came out of the woodwork. Even friends and business acquaintances have approached me asking if I need investment! Where were they when I really needed them? Where were they when there was a higher risk? The banks manage risk but they are not all monsters. They do not want you to be exposed to so much debt. There is a chance you will lose everything. They do not want your house if that is what you are underwriting the loan with. They just want you to risk as much as them. Banks have formulas in place now. There is no relationship and you cannot build trust with anybody. If you do, it's academic because your point of contact does not have responsibility anyway.

Of course, Thinking Space now has history and assets of its own, so it could borrow in its own right. The risk is reduced but there are now more tests and risks because as the company grows, there has to be a balance of investment in development, investment in people and the ability to take opportunities. Risk is everywhere.

My company is reasonably averse to risk. We have gambled a few times but all the biggest risks were taken by me in the first two years.

The first risk I took was probably handing over a cheque for £12,000 to a guy in a pub! In May 2003, I designed 12 aluminium profiles. This was the first design of what is now called the CORE system. I had asked my operations director to produce them in CAD and then started sending them to companies for quotes. Within a week I realised I simply did not have enough money. The good thing was that in 2003, personal borrowing was easy, especially when you could get a credit card within around 15 minutes of application. This was risky. This was a personal debt I was building up that at its height was around £27,000. After 14 months of the company being in business, that was the moment of maximum risk and debt. That does not include the fact I did not pay myself a penny for the first 18 months.

The pub story came about because I was working from home in a dining room, so not a place to meet. When the prices came back from the aluminium suppliers in regard to the custom extrusions I needed to have made, they all wanted me to purchase 500kg of each profile shape. That is six tonnes of aluminium that in theory should connect together! I could not afford that amount. The guy who I met in the pub worked for the only company who would let me buy 250kg batches. This halved my risk. I then worked hard to see what profiles I could live without and then placed my first order. Because my company was new, there was no offer of payment terms. Full payment with order was the only deal. I asked for a test piece of each extrusion and the guy said, "Yes, sure, each piece will be 250kg's of stock."

The profiles took eight weeks to produce, in which time I had to find a workshop and buy equipment to cut and drill the shapes. This was good positive pressure and risk; a deadline helps focus. The designer helped me find a shed (marketing later called it a barn) and I will always remember when my first saws and equipment arrived as I waited for the stock to be delivered. The most nerve-racking day of my business life was when two tonnes of aluminium arrived. All my money wrapped in cardboard. I have to say it did not look like £12,000 worth! Cutting a piece in half and seeing if they would join together with my steel anchor system took another 24 hours.

My friend's dad, Mr Sebborn, had a lathe and turned two anchors I had drawn, machining them around the profile core holes to get them working. It took further two weeks to perfect the connectors because the part had to bend and not break, material research added some time but the system worked. It was definitely not perfect and it took about three months to further test the materials and get them working even better. But it worked and that moment of risk passed.

Since then, there have been other moments that have kept me awake over the years but more to do with a lack of sales. A couple of recessions cranked up the stress but the main exposure to risk was avoided because of a decision we did not take, which I greatly regretted at the time.

Around three years into the business, one of my main competitors went bust. They were based less than ten miles from us and at the time it was a great boost for Thinking Space as we went after their clients. There were three of us at the time and overnight we doubled in size. We took on two of their managers became an agent for one of the products they distributed and purchased their data base of customers from the receiver. We grew from one barn to two and then three within 12 months and the business showed its first profit (Yes, it took two years of losses before the company made a profit).

So where was the lack of risk? What we should have done was buy them out and move into their premises, keeping everything live. We could have taken the staff and would have maintained the customer database. The business would have gone for 90k to 600k over night but my balls were not big enough! I did not want that debt of purchase and the management time was too big for me then.

We took a calculated risk every time we relocated. Commercial property rent is a real challenge and that is partly because I have yet to meet a landlord I wanted to have a drink with. I really hope that is changing now.

Buying a business some years later also carried a degree of risk but this was in a different way. This was a risk to my reputation. At the time we were established with the management team consisting of myself as MD and two other shareholding directors. One was the commercial director and the other was the operations director. These two directors are (or were) more risk averse so the

45

idea of purchasing another business was not on their radar and I had to convince them it was the way to go. My reputation was on the line when we negotiated and took on the business. It definitely did not turn out the way I had intended but it did make us money and as a team of directors we learnt a lot together. I guess to measure the success and experience, I am sure all three of us would do it again if the right business was selected. So is my reputation intact, not sure I had one to start with but having thick skin is what you learn to grow anyway.

What is interesting is that some ten years later, my fellow directors are keen to find new acquisitions. We have learnt and gained experience and can perhaps manage the risk more. Either that or our balls have just naturally got bigger!

Experience always helps. The more times you do something, the easier it becomes and both the stress levels and risks are reduced. Meeting important customers in the early days is always hard as the risk is high but so is the need for business. Now we are more professional and although we still need the work, we now have a number of processes in place to remove risk and help manage the customer's expectations.

So in summary, it is not really about your appetite for risk, it is how you select what risk to take and how comfortable you are with it. Nobody wants to fail and if you are too stressed, you will not function to your full capacity, you will not make the correct decisions, you will probably suffer from a lack of sleep and become unwell and you do not want that.

Always try to manage the risk and understand your limits in terms of the risks you are happy to take. It is not easy to walk away from something, especially if you have been involved in a risk that has increased or grown over time.

Risk is always about perception. I am a positive person and generally an optimist. I would always suggest, if you can, to surround yourself with positive people. It is fascinating to me that I consider the two most positive people I know are both accountants. Generally, accountants are risk averse, so I wonder if that is one of the reasons for their positive outlooks. I will ask both Graham and Hayley (my accountants) this question and perhaps report back in the next book!

Chapter Nine
Right Person, Right Box

This is tough to get right so you need to think and plan this at the start of your journey. I am not the sort of guy that enjoys conflict and for me, this part of the job is shitty because this is all about managing people and ensuring the right person is in the right box. This may include having to let them go if they do not fit either the role they are in or the culture of the company.

In the early years this is vital because when you start, you cannot afford six people for six jobs. You need someone who can do a bit of all six (I never said this was easy). The thing that nobody tells you is once you get bigger, a 'jack of all trades and master of none' is the opposite of what you need.

As your business grows, the people needs you have change. This could mean your top person in the early days, the one that did everything and ran around with you doing all they could to grow the business over time, becomes the type of person your business not only does not need, but the type of person that is now doing more harm than good!

I know this from bitter experience because the person we had an issue with was the main man, literally because it was bloody me! You see, I am not a process person. I am a hands on, get-it-done-and-help-the-customer type of manager. This is fine when there are two, three, or four people in the business because everyone knows who is doing what. But, it is no good when you are 30 or more people. It then becomes impossible for everyone to know what everyone else is doing. You then need processes set up and for me, the challenge was that this was not my skill set at all.

You need to evolve yourself or create a new box/role for yourself. From a personal point of view I found this theory was easy to understand and agree with but difficult to do. I simply went back to the box I was good at, which was sales. I knew what I was good at, so put myself in the correct box. The challenge was more of a personal ego issue. I was the boss and got used to leading people. I had to let go to some degree because although I knew I was a good motivator and had the vision of what the future of the business looked like, I needed to hand control of some of the staff to others that had more of a talent for it. I am still very much the driver and motivator but the teams within the company require process and consistency. I feel a 'lead by example' approach is important, so what each department deserved was a manager that knew and followed an agreed process and set examples within it. What they do not need is a guy who, perhaps, considers processes slow down service levels and flexibility (to some degree I still believe they do).

All joking aside, structure is one of the keys to growth and if that is not enough of a motivator, then good company systems make the company more valuable and if you are not such a hands-on owner when the business is up for sale, then the firm is worth more still.

This chapter, however, is not about the business owner breaking away, it is about spotting when a person is not in the right box and then doing something about it. I have three examples for you, one good, one not so good and one that made me cry (I did say this was sodding difficult).

James is one of our managers here at Thinking Space, a top guy who I value along with all our management team. James did not start as a manager like most of us with a small growing business, he has evolved with it. He joined us as a sales guy. James had come from a car dealership where he worked in customer service and wanted to make the transition into sales. We thought we could mould him into a Thinking Space man. James is a good communicator but he had an issue that took us a year to work out. James is a details man and found it tough to delegate (we are working on that even today). What this meant was that his commitment to each individual customer limited the number of customers he could support at any given time. This was compounded by the fact that James is a perfectionist, a subject we will cover later in the book. It was limiting our growth. Remember, this was a time when we could not afford six people in six job roles. How could we afford a guy whose style meant he could not manage the multiple communication requirements of the sales function? However, when we gave James a single dedicated action or challenge, he embraced it, took control and got the job done. Clearly James was in the wrong box. We did not want to let him go as he fitted the Thinking Space person profile and culture we were developing. With James fully involved, we moved him to a more office based internal sales function working with customers already identified by the field team. This meant that the number of customers he would need to deal with decreased because he was expected to spend more time with each one. This was the correct box for James. It worked out well and James later helped the business achieve its ISO 9001 status and is now the manager of a complete product range.

It can sometimes take a while to work out that people are in the wrong box or that the box has changed shape or size! When you do understand this 'box' analogy, you can then understand that two things must be managed. When you create a role or box and recruit, you will often find the box will change around the person. It is vital that the key objectives of the role or box are still fulfilled. Do not change a box to fit the person, otherwise you could end up with people working in areas that do not support the objectives of the company. I have touched on this previously.

As a manager, you also need to make sure the box's all fit together. No box is independent, in fact each role and function within a business is a piece of the jigsaw that makes up the final picture of the company. The best companies have all the parts fitting and as the overall picture of the company changes, the pieces can be changed to match it.

My next example does not have such a happy ending. After 14 years of growth, it was decided we wanted to introduce some new blood and create a senior role in the management team. We wanted to bring someone in with experience and knowledge of another larger sector of business. Our new head of production had all the right experience and history of managing a larger operation. There were a very pleasant person but what they did not have was the 'Thinking Space' culture within them. I did not know it was so important until we had to ask them to leave. They were not hands on. They were very much a systems/process desk person, which is what we wanted but we also needed someone to champion and adopt the culture of our management style and the business. As it turns out, it affected both the performance and feeling throughout the business. In fact, it was not until we had received the resignation of a valuable member of the team that we realised we had to make a change. It was not me who noticed the issues but our operations director. It was a tough call for Paul because it was his idea to employ this type of manager. I have always respected Paul's judgement and I did even more when he held his hand up and came to the conclusion that he had made a mistake and had to ask them to leave. Some decisions that you have to make in business are educated risks and gambles rather than simple yes/no decisions. Often you do not know if they are right until months or years later. I can say now that years later it was the correct thing to do. Sometimes, there are truly grey areas, but you do just need to make a decision. We knew and agreed we did need new managers to join the team. We wanted new blood and senior staff that came with knowledge and experience but at that time is was just too soon. Letting people go is quite simply the shittiest job but it has to be done, otherwise your business could fail. I will talk about this in more detail in another chapter. In this case the decision was the correct one and the business benefited from it.

So, several times I mentioned culture. What do I mean by 'Thinking Space' culture? Early in our business development stage, the management team wrote down what our core values should be and we all signed up to them. The idea was to create a team spirit of one that cares and to create a culture of learning and development. Our values also include how we treat each other and respect one another.

My final example involves a friend of mine, who we took on to sell a new product from Germany. She was hard working, fitted in to the team culture and was totally committed but it just did not work. We did everything to try and get the product selling into a mature market. It was a tough day when we had to let her go and I remember the conversation we had to this day. This was not a case of her not fitting into a box or the box not fitting within the team but simply a case that the box had to go.

I have promised myself to this day never to employ someone I was not prepared to let go if things do not work out. My top tip here is, before you offer someone a job, make sure you are capable of letting them go, even if they have done nothing wrong themselves. Sometimes, that is just business and it is a reason why a lot of people either do not employ family or live to regret it.

When you work through the growing stages of your business, think about every role you fill and how that job will change next year or the year after. Is the person in front of you capable of being the right person for that box in 12–18 months? Are they going to be able to develop for the next five years? Sometimes, what makes it harder is you must compromise with the person you select. You simply might not attract the person you need or in our case could not afford the skills, meaning you need to develop the person and the role. I would use the football team analogy here. My team are Saints, currently in the premier league. A good season is mid table but they achieve this by purchasing young players with potential and getting as much out of them as they can in terms of performance before they head off to bigger clubs. The advantage a football team has is that when the player leaves the team. They are sold, so the training and investment is rewarded by way of a big cheque.

Sadly, in business, we cannot invoice a new employer because they have taken our top player! So what should you do? In some business cultures employees are not valued and you will see managers repress talent or not invest in training. My approach is one of development and investment. We always strive to run a business where we care for our staff and do what we can to make their time with us good for them and for us. We are a small company, so sometimes we cannot offer the fantastic salaries and packages that larger firms can. What we have done is worked hard on our culture and our duty of care for the people that choose to work with us. I never let my team forget that we should be grateful that the staff here have a choice where they work and I am fully aware how hard it is to attract good people.

Some people do evolve and it is the perk of a growing company when you see how far people have come in their career development. The other side of this is you could end up with someone who quickly does not fit. This is not an easy part of the job but is so important.

My final word regarding culture and the 'right person in the right box' is to action your decisions as compassionately as you can, be formal, follow a process and be sincere, not only when you ask someone to leave but also when they decide to go, even if you are disappointed they are leaving.

Chapter Ten
My Way, or the Highway

Not sure this chapter heading could be any clearer. Hardly cryptic, is it! This is not all about driving your values and beliefs through the business. It is about more than that. Being the boss is the loneliest job ever and you must have a lot of self-belief. You must be able to stand your ground and drive through the business what you believe to be right. The trouble is, when you have this attitude (which you do need), it does not always come over as the friendliest way to work, so this heading is more about your confidence in what you are trying to do rather than about you stamping your feet and bossing people around. Be in no doubt that your true standards will come through from the top, and over time, if you try to fake it, this will show. When the business is larger, there is opportunity to hide, but it is much better to live by the values you create. To make it even more difficult, if you want to generate a good positive culture within the business, your attitude to people and the way you communicate will be the backbone of it.

Let us start from the beginning. You start a company, it is just you and that is good because although you have to do everything, the big plus is you know that it is being done and it is done the way you want it. You have decided what the priorities are. You have selected what job gets done first and how well to do each job. Communication is easy because you know everything that is going on. When you talk to suppliers and customers, you dictate deliveries, deadlines and the standards you want. The time has come to recruit and you have someone new joining the business. The challenge here is like meeting someone who has lived on their own for a long time. I had a girlfriend who was great fun but the challenge was she had lived on her own for many years before we got together. It is not a deal breaker at all or even a bad thing ,but it is a challenge getting used to someone else messing up your stuff and being involved with the way you live. In a relationship you learn to compromise or, I guess, you end the relationship!

In business you must get a balance of getting things done how you want them done and accepting that some things are not what you exactly want but are acceptable.

As you can imagine, when you have one employee, you can get them on board with how you want things done. You can perhaps do that with the first four or five new employees but as the business grows, you will find that your staff will have their own standards and new employees may not be learning how to do things your way unless this is documented. So the key word here is process. If you document and create standards and processes for your business, things will be easier. It is the same way with culture (well nearly), what we did was create a set of values and linked these to our mission statement. These documents were then linked to the company's five-year plan. We also created an employee handbook, which not only details what we will do as an employer but lays out our expectations of each employee which in turn is linked to culture. Understanding that everything is linked is important. You cannot say one thing and do something else; it is pointless.

That is easy, yes? No, it is sodding impossible because when you start, you have to work out what process works, remember, chances are you have only done it a dozen times yourself. In addition to that, a process that is great for five people is useless for 35. What we have also not factored in is that, documenting a process is at the bottom of your to do list when you are running a new business. I never said this stuff was easy, did I? It is not complicated but it takes time and needs to be completed in stages.

There is nobody in the business that will have your drive and passion for the company. That does not mean you will not have people who care. Just because they are doing things differently does not make their way is the wrong way. However, every now and again you must stand up and be the decision maker. I have been at this over 18 years, running several firms. I guess I must make major decisions within the business around once a year but small decisions that shape the way we work are made daily.

When you start your business, big decisions are made every day but as your processes develop and as your team get more confident, things change for the better and others with more experience in specific areas make decisions that affect them locally. Things such as which clients get credit, this is now process driven, accounts carry out a credit check, they score their history and follow a process to decide. The process even has a level of credit before I am asked to get involved and make a final decision. Any client, who is late in paying, will be flagged, they will lose their credit option and the process will start again.

My decisions might have greater ramifications, but they are certainly not any more important than the ones taken 18 years ago. The advantage now is we have experience to fall back on. The business has history and because we now have a team of managers, we can now discuss some of the decisions made.

I said earlier how lonely running a firm can be and this was what surprised me the most when running Thinking Space. Everyone in your team quite rightly must look out for themselves to some degree and they will be able to make decisions that fall within their job role, but it is you and only you that must stand there and make the big decisions, e.g. firing someone, new business acquisitions or relocating the company. These are massive decisions that affect everyone within the organisation.

One constant issue for me was when I took on a business partner fairly early, he pushed me for more money all the time. I think for the first five years of working together, every month there was a comment or a dig about money. At the time, it was torture. Was he about to leave because of money? Could the business afford to pay him more and if he got more, should I get the same? Eventually, I grew in confidence and realised he just pushed every month out of habit. I devised a structure around performance and made my first corporate decision that no employee was going to be paid more than me! This was challenging because when Paul asked for more, I knew that the request was going to be double what he wanted because I was going to give myself the same. To be fair, Paul was and is worth every penny, even if at the time he was a pain in the arse!

So, we are clear that you must stand up and be able to tell someone they are not doing a task how you want it to be done. But, what if you have demonstrated how you want something done only to return later to see the person has done it their way but the end result is actually better than how you would have done it!

After we had been in business about a year, I was building a console and it was the most complicated so far in the company's short history. I was using connectors that were not ideal, so I had to work out new drilling angles and mitre joints as I went. I managed to finish it but I have to say it was not pretty. With no time and little choice, I was getting ready to start talking about the installation with the client. At the same time I had advertised for my first fitter, who would be a full-time employee, so a big step. Along came Pete! I interviewed four people, all from different mechanical backgrounds and probably made one of the best recruiting decisions of my career. Now do not get me wrong. Pete was not (and is not) perfect but at that time and even now, 18 years later, we still work perfectly together.

I showed Pete around the barn, made him a cup of tea, and talked through this complicated job (that I had made a hash of). Pete was from a marine background and could turn his hand to anything. He did not want the stress levels of a big business and he looked at my barn as a small home workshop. I offered him the job there and then but had to explain that I did not have a contract of employment. There was no HR manual, nothing like an employee handbook and my health and safety training consisted of me telling him to 'be careful'. He accepted the challenge and as we drank our tea together, he turned to me and with a smile on his face said, "I will stay with you until a proper job comes along, Wayne." The first thing he did was strip the console apart that I had just put together and he rebuilt it. It did mean that I was a little bit late in delivering the job but it did set a precedence in that. It is better to be right rather than on time. It is true to this day that people will remember the quality long after any delays in delivery (we do now have a good reputation for good quality and delivery).

Pete set out the process and standards for the early consoles. He never actually wrote them down but for years, all new employees spent a few months working with Pete, so they could learn his processes and ways to manufacturer.

Pete would like to tinker with things. He made jigs and fixtures, fixed lights, un-blocked the toilets and kept himself busy when I had nothing for him to do during quiet moments. One afternoon about nine months in, he was cleaning up and he asked if he needed to start looking for another job because I had nothing for him to do. It cemented our relationship and taught me something more about communication. I was confident that the pipeline of work was filling and we would soon be busy but I had not told Pete. So I made him a cuppa and filled him in, assuring him there was work to come and that I was in fact waiting for an order to arrive that day. There was no way he was going anywhere. What I had not done was tell him what the status of the business was! I had not communicated to him how we were doing, if we were making money or what the future plan was. From that day forward, another process was created. We had a monthly meeting with the whole business. Yes, both of us. We had a cup tea but this time with a biscuit and I told him what was going on, what had happened and what to expect to happen in the next month.

Nowadays, Thinking Space holds a team meeting every month which includes everyone within the business. Of course, now we are bigger, each manager reports on performance. We talk safety, projects and what VIP visitor's we can expect in the factory. The meeting includes the company's performance, both good and bad and we make sure all the information is concise and easy to understand.

Pete should have retired two years ago but is still with us, although now part time, he remains our longest standing employee. I guess this had turned into a proper job, after all ! What is interesting from a management angle is, nowadays, we cannot afford to have another Pete in the business because the box we had for Pete is not a priority . We now need people that build consoles and can do that quickly and efficiently.

Pete once described himself to me as a tractor, he said, "I'm not going to be fast but I'm going to keep going." He was unsupervised 90% of the time but now we cannot afford for a fitter to fix lights and toilets. We have contractors to do this because it does not affect the production flow. Perhaps your business like ours is perfect with one Pete but several Pete's would be an issue.

Be aware that Pete was not perfect because he refused to go to site and install the consoles. I think he did one or two in the early days but he did not want to deal with customers and to be honest his efforts and willingness to accommodate a client could mean we spent time on site work that was not paid. When on site, we needed to complete the work to an agreed standard, get out and get paid. We needed to get back because there would be another project waiting for us. Pete could have spent an extra two days on every project if given freedom to do so. That is not a criticism, it is how he worked. My job was to manage that because my job is to make a profit.

It took time but as the roles became more specialised, people in the workshop, sales and project managers started to connect better together. We will have the odd conflict or confusion but that is where one of us has to step in and make a decision. The goal is to empower people to decide and we are still working towards that.

Chapter Eleven
Don't Follow

For me, this is one of the toughest things to do. There are many basic guidelines when starting up a company and I have included as much as I can in this book but for me, this is the toughest.

Trying 'not to follow' affects the culture of the business. Remember, this is written by a mechanical guy who started in his mum and dad's dining room and not an ex-finance well-read business coach. I am no expert and am only talking based on my experience and that of business friends I have worked with. As a mechanical person, the ideas around creativity and business culture are not easy for me to embrace but it is linked to this chapter just like culture is interwoven within all the subjects. Trying to be more creative and less mechanical is one of the challenges I work on every day. If you can introduce a culture of change, innovation and a determination not to follow, you will be forward thinking as a business.

Trying 'not to follow' is all about working out how to be just a little different. As a commercial customer led firm, we are constantly working out new approaches to 'wow' our customers in what we offer. One reason 'not to follow' is about appealing to customers and developing ideas for marketing that make us stand out from the crowd.

'Not following' is another angle of commercial attack, which will help you when you are in a competitive market and let's face it, who isn't! Let me give you an example. We attend a major international show each year in Madrid. The exhibition format is standard, three or four halls of products and services with potential clients visiting, looking and gathering data. I am not going to talk about show stands and marketing here but being a bit different has an effect and in Madrid we have hit the jackpot three years running. Let me explain how.

As the exhibition became bigger, the organiser wanted to keep all the technical furniture companies in the same hall. Nothing unusual there until they re-designed the layout one year, wanting us all together in one corner. I could see the logic. It would be easy to direct someone who wanted a console but with our limited budget, it would have not been possible for us to compete with the larger stands of established companies. So we kept to our usual area and worked hard 'not to follow' by making the booth bright and original. We had quite an argument with the organiser but in the end we were allowed to stay where we were. Do not be afraid to push back.

This was a risk. We sell on the technology, the solution and engineering. The show came and we were nervous. We were on the opposite side of the hall to everyone else. Would visitors find us? Would we get noticed? It turned out fine and what made it better was that the three main competitors going head to head as expected. They used marketing consultants and exhibition designers to create new stands. The latest style and colour trend at the time was very white, clean lines with black detail. On the first day of the show we walked across to check out the competition. All three main stands were large black and white designs with lots of white worktops. The marketing departments had done their job and all three firms looked identical! You could not tell one company from another. Even the products were the same designs. All the companies did the same for three years. One has now gone bust.

In contrast, we had bursts of colour. This was definitely not on trend. We tried to innovate and show something different to draw attention in a positive way. I am not suggesting gimmicks, I am not a fan of what used to be called 'booth bait', where a pretty lady or guy reels people in. I remember attending a security show one year where a padlock company had built a stand that looked like a dungeon and had employed ladies in bondage type outfits. I tracked down the sales manager in a bar one evening to get his thoughts if it worked. He told me he was resigning the next week! It was not the image he wanted, the booth was seedy and attracted spectators rather than customers. It was the idea of an aging director who was out of touch with modern approaches and he did not want to be associated with a company like that! During the event itself, we had customers asking if we could provide some of the innovations shown on our competitor's booths, not unusual but what was interesting was that they couldn't remember on which stand they had seen it as they all looked the same. Combine this information with the increased enquiries we achieved at the event, proved that our approach was a success.

In the early days with a limited budget, innovation is not easy and as the company grows and introduces more processes and standards, change gets harder, because it becomes slower to develop. But if you can create the right culture, the desire to lead and become innovative becomes part of the firms DNA. I am not a creative genius, I do not have a team of dedicated people even now working on this, but what we do have is the desire to be different and to solve problems created by customers. The balance and challenge is when you lead, you are taking risk. It might be un-tested and people might not want it. As the company grows, you can research to verify the change and investment but I have to be honest if you are close to the customers and talk to them about their requirements, you have all the information you need.

If possible, try to chat to your competitors' customers, try to work out why they use them and not you? In the first ten years of my company, most of our innovation came from the development of what was already out there. We would strive to put our own spin on existing solutions, either from a design angle or perhaps a marketing approach. Either way, always working out how we could make it better. I still visit trade shows for domestic and office furniture products, looking for ideas that I can introduce into my furniture. I look at kitchen units to see how drawers and doors are developed to see if we can use them and bring them to a new market? This is not expensive, just some time and travel costs but for me it is so important.

The desire to lead should also drive the manufacturing development. Let us be honest, it is cool to be customer focused but much cooler to make lots of money! Constantly work on process and product changes, that will also help your efficiency in design and production. Push for change and work at getting people to expect it. This is all very difficult because product development can be expensive and slow. One challenge I have had to come to terms with now the business is bigger, is how development has slowed. Without a dedicated development team, the day-to-day work can easily take priority with my managers. It is also difficult to get positive buy in. One of my directors only sees what development costs and does not consider the longer game or the value of more cosmetic improvements. To be honest, 'jam tomorrow' is more my responsibility but you do need everyone on board if you can.

Today, the business is investing heavily into both product development and ideas that are not typically used in our sectors. I would recommend this approach but it takes time and when you start, time is not always available. Try to push hard as well as being pragmatic. Also remember that a lot of this is 'jam tomorrow', so get the balance.

One of the benchmarks I set myself is to be on one of our exhibition stands and be able to show a customer what is new that year. If I can do that, I know we are still moving forward. Sometimes, it is just a website change but we are always trying to make it something that is useful to the customer and is perhaps more tangible.

There is something called 'perceived value', which is worth understanding. This is all about when the user thinks the new innovation or solution is expensive but actually the cost to manufacture or supply is relatively low in comparison to what they are willing to pay for it. Over the years we have got better at increasing our 'perceived value'. I cannot give you a direct example from my own company because it is commercially sensitive. We do not want the competition to know what we can do cheaply and what is painful.

Leading is great for marketing, it is an excuse to reach out to your existing customers with legitimate news. You can approach industry press with news and launch the change at events. The big plus for me is the affect it has on our team. When the staff here see us striving to change and improve, they become motivated. The opportunity to work on innovation is also a break from the day-to-day work. From a personal perspective, I enjoy the changes we make to what we can offer the client. It is also important for a small company to have this attitude from the top.

Never forget that people also want to work for companies that are proactive, developing and growing. I am sure it helps retain staff and attract them in the first place. It always makes me smile when I see jobs advertised by companies, who claim they are 'market leaders' in whatever they do. Not sure how this is defined but they use the term to attract good people.

Never worry about the competition, copying what you do when it comes to innovation, for me, that is the sign that you are doing things right. Take it as a nod of respect. When you start working internationally, you will soon see your products and ideas being ripped off. As a small firm, the idea of protecting the brand is relatively futile. I do not have the money, desire or time to try and sue a company in India or China. Protect ideas as long as you can but do not lose sleep over it. Just come up with another one, a better one.

When trying to lead and gather ideas, try to do it with a degree of respect. You do not have to exactly copy something you see. Always try to improve it and put your own spin on it. In addition to this, do not do anything dodgy and remember, the other people in your sector are competitors and not the enemy. Set some moral and ethical standards for your team and the business. We recently had a sales guy came to us for a job, he joined us from a competitor, stating his driving factor was our reputation and how we worked. It can only be a good thing if a competitor holds you in high regard because it is a clear indication the rest of the market do too.

One true trait of an entrepreneur, which I clearly have, is to never be satisfied. By not following and by leading, you are always trying to improve. If you drive continued development within your business, things will happen.

Chapter Twelve
The Yes Man

I use the term 'man' figuratively in this chapter, it can absolutely be a woman.

When the business first started and there was only a couple of us involved, I was on a mission to win work and get busy. Paul Atkins was working with me and all he would hear was me on the phone saying yes to every request. Yes, sir, we can do that. I will take care of that for you, no problem! Paul had to turn his hand to everything from console building to painting and decorating and even carpet fitting if I had sold it as part of the project. Perhaps, it is profitable and possible when the site is around the corner but not so easy when it is 250 miles away or on another continent!

There was method in my madness, such low overheads meant there was still margin in the work, even if it was miles away. We already know that 'cash is king', especially in the early days, it is all about the 'bread and butter' but as the business grows and we start spending on staff, premises, cars and machinery, we need to have better margins and to focus on what makes us money.

If you can work out what your 'sweet spot' is and make it the centre of your sales and marketing, then you are on to a winner. The sweet spot is simply the product or solution that makes the most money. Chances are it is your main product/service, it is what you are good at and what the firm is geared up for. There are some caveats, of course, if nobody wants to buy what you are good at, then revert to chapter one! If the market is not big enough or there are other regulatory factors you cannot manage, then perhaps it is a non-starter.

What is interesting is it took a long time to work out exactly where we made the most money, we were too busy and not on it during the early days. It is not easy to calculate until you have some experience and you grow a little. For example, we provide consoles into five different markets but if these markets do not have their own budgets, how can you tell which one gives the best return on investment?

We got there in the end and now focus on providing the solution that makes the most money. As we repeatedly won this work, we got even better at it, becoming more efficient made us more money. There is a challenge here, if you only produce/provide the single thing that makes money, then a change in the market force can expose you to risk. For example, if you run a company selling various fire extinguishers but the one that makes you the best margin is full of foam, you should focus on selling more foam units. Sounds really simple. However, do not rule out the other extinguishers from your offer, just be aware which one you really want to sell because you will have issues if a regulation changes and foam is no longer acceptable! On the other hand, if you are only known in the market for foam and it becomes compulsory, then you have struck gold. OK, so this example is extreme and hopefully you are monitoring regulation changes, so will already be in the know and reacting to this. What if you could influence the law? What if you could change regulation so that your product is the one people must have? Hopefully, this is not something that you would ever consider as this is called corruption. We will talk about that later.

One thing that has worked for me has been increasing the 'sweet spot' or the products with maximum margin. Being a 'yes man' taught me a lot of things. Most of it was not good but I learnt what to avoid if nothing else. It gave us scope and knowledge and over time, we developed as a business, so that the skills increased to widen the amount/variety of work we could supply that generated a good margin. With a larger 'sweet spot', we could pick up more work. If this is taken to the extreme and you start another 'sweet spot' somewhere else, it is called diversification! As a small business let us hope you do not have to do this early on. It is high risk and usually needs high investment.

I am not only always looking for new solutions and products to add to our range but I am constantly developing our existing offer to increase the 'sweet spot'. The other angle is to get the existing solution or offer into another sector or market. Now this could be a business sector that we are new to but it could also be a completely new market in a new country.

Based on the above, you would now think that I no longer say 'yes' but this is the interesting thing, I say 'yes' just as much now but for the right reasons. If I am asked to provide other items which are not our core product, I will definitely still include them in the quote but show them as optional extras so that the client has the option whether or not to have them. I make it clear to the customer that it is not our core business and we may be slightly higher on price than a local provider. We have found that some of our customers prefer to use one supplier and have one person to deal with, so it is worth something to them.

As a sales guy, I am always likely to say 'yes' if it is going to increase the order value but this has caused some problems on a couple of projects. One being in the north of England, where we agreed to change the lighting in an old building, where the control room was being moved to. The prime contractor said they were 'busy' and would we take it on. It seemed simple and as ever I was keen to say 'yes'. There had previously been issues with a contractor working on site, who did not get on with the local authority, H&S Inspector, who was on site daily. The contractor had taken some risks, which meant the client was being very strict. Because of this, there were some very tight constraints, some of which were un-realistic. There are regulations that require a working platform rather than a ladder when working above a certain height. The ceiling was 2", too high for a ladder, and the H&S person was demanding we build a working platform to change the lighting. This was fair enough but he would then not let us into the roof space to install the light fittings as the roof space did not have any lighting of its own. A chicken and egg situation! This was how we found out why we had been asked to fit the lights! The main contractor knew about this conundrum and just wanted to pass the buck. Saying 'yes' does not always work and having this happen to us a couple of times has made us more cautious. I will not tell you how we got around it but all I will say is, sometimes, it is easier to beg for forgiveness rather than to ask for permission!

Surrounding yourself with people that say 'yes' makes you feel nice, might massage your ego, but do nothing for the business or your own development. If you employ a lot of untrained, inexperienced people, who are not confident in taking a different approach, you will have a lot of 'yes' answers to things you do. If you get things right and these people grow in confidence through experience and the training you provide, they will start standing up to you and start questioning your decisions. It is really enlightening when a manager tells you, "You are wrong," it takes a lot of courage for them to do so. My top tip is to not be defensive when this first happens! Be proud of the moment, use your skills as a manager to encourage that person to do it regularly but still try and get your own way if you can, ha.

I was very compliant as a child and young adult and I was determined to make sure my children were not like that. It is a great moment and I would suggest it is a coming of age when one of your children disagrees with you for what I would call a legitimate reason. I am not talking about cleaning their bedroom or doing homework, I am talking about conversations over dinner. My daughter and I have different views on politics, in fact, they are closer than she thinks but I enjoy the debates and I love her passion and willing to challenge what I say. Katie likes a bit of confrontation. What is interesting to me is my son attacks things differently. His approach is more conducive. Adam uses his charm to get us where he wants us. Perhaps, I, and we can learn something from both of them.

Chapter Thirteen
Keep the Door Open

Hardly an unusual statement, but not always easy to do. There are several reasons for this and I have a few pointers for you if you are going to say, "My door is always open."

I run my companies in a way that is inclusive and during the early days that was easy. With only two or three employees, you tend to see and hear everything and because you are involved in everything, you quite simply micro-manage the business. Now that is OK and something you can do if you want to keep everything within your control but micromanaging is hardly management as you are telling people exactly what you want and when you want it. If you want full disclosure and to know everything that goes on, you do not really have a choice. This can be challenging if and when you want to step back. You need to know that I am actually quite lazy and the last thing I want to do is work long hours. So to grow, you need trust, you also need to introduce good solid processes and then you have to live by them. What has this got to do with leaving the door open? Read on…

By telling your team, "My door is always open," there is an opportunity for anyone to come in at any time! That is the point right unless you say it but don't mean it! When someone comes to see you, you should drop everything and stop and listen. Unless you are happy to do this, you do not truly have an open-door policy. It is not supposed to be 'by appointment only'. Whatever you do, you cannot dismiss the employee's thoughts because then the door might as well be shut! Remember, it could have taken a lot of courage for the person to come up the stairs and walk into the office of the MD.

There are huge benefits to the open-door policy but it can also lead to some problems. People may come to influence you and avoid either conflict with their line manager or just as bad want to by-pass a process you have in place that they should follow. You are probably wondering why they have come to see you rather than their line manager. Why they feel the need to talk to the MD? These are all questions you are not allowed to ask!

I remember one of our workshop guys coming to see me to make a suggestion to improve one or our production processes. Brilliant, it was great that he felt confident to do this and I praised him but at the same time I was wondering why he had not gone to his line manager? Did he not trust his manager? Or did he just want to blow air up the skirt of the MD to show how good he was? Maybe it was neither of these but it made me realise I needed to have a process in place that allowed the employee to speak with both the MD and their line manager. That way, when I fed everything back to the correct manager, they would not be upset because they were bypassed and I would not be down grading the person who came in to see me.

There may be times when an employee comes to see you because they have an issue with another member of staff or their line manager. They have come to you deliberately to avoid the company process so it is likely to be sensitive and what will always be true is that it is important to them. The important thing is to follow your policy. This will include writing everything down. It shows that you are listening, you value what the person is saying and you want to make sure you do not miss anything. There are books on body language and ways to show that you are listening and paying attention but writing things down is a cool way to stay engaged and to let the person talking think what they are saying is important to you. Try not to say too much but advise them of the process and what action you are going to take. Do not make any promises without all of the information. Think of the analogy of a child asking Mum for something when they do not get the answer they want, they go off and ask Dad. Quite often there is a reason why Mum said "no."

Always summarise the conversation at the end to show that you have understood what has been said.

I have been asked by an employee if they can they have a chat with me off the record. Do not answer that question. Everything said to you is 100% 'ON' the record. You are the judge. You are the referee and as the managing director, CEO, founder or whatever title you give yourself. You are the most senior and most accountable person in the business. In most countries you will be the one who is sued, taken to court or investigated for any business irregularities. Even if you have other shareholders and stake holders, it is the one with the biggest shares who will be in the dock. Nothing is said to you off the record. It is why you get the bigger salary. The risk and reward is at your feet, so never forget that.

When it comes to the open-door policy, try to formalise things a little, try not to become the social secretary because people need to understand you are busy. The idea is to create good communication and transparency within the business, so work hard on how you communicate information and how you exchange information you have been given by others.

The final thought I would like to include within this section is not so much about an open-door policy but more perhaps about a 'social conversation' policy.

I have worked with the two directors here for over 18 years and regard them as friends as well as colleagues. Outside work, the three of us can talk frankly and freely and when it is just the three of us, the conversation can easily roll in and out of business. It is one of the major advantages of having business partners. It took a few years for Paul Roberts to grow into his role and to build the confidence and trust to speak freely but we do that now.

The challenge changes when you socialise with employees that are not on the same managerial level. This is where there is a link with the open-door policy. You must remember you are always the boss even when the company has social events. For example, each year we try to run a family day, where we invite employees and their families on a day out. I find it interesting that I am often introduced to a family member as the Boss and not as Wayne! As I have said before, there are no 'off the record' conversations because in that environment, you are the top man. You will be watched for the way you interact and the way you respond to people. You can also use it to your advantage. I always take my children to the family days and interact as I normally would be by being a little silly. People then see you as a little more normal and you can break down barriers. I have made mistakes during a couple of Christmas parties. I have perhaps drunk a little more than I should have but I do not think I have knowingly made a fool of myself, although I can't remember!

Socialising with people you pay is not easy but what if they are also family? I have both my sister and nephew working within the business. To set the scene, note that I am very close to my sister. I trust her with my life and we do socialise together as brothers and sisters do. Losing our parents relatively young and having both gone through marriage break ups has only made us closer. The downside is that from time to time, she does 'bend my ear' and I must listen. On the plus side, I can be myself. I am not the boss when we are together because she is. I have no problem with this, not sure what my fellow director's views are but for me, Tina being part of the business is a massive plus. My advice would be to proceed with caution. I would not suggest you work in an office with someone you live with. I know many couples who have worked together and some who met at work. Just proceed with caution and make sure it works for you. I would not rule it out but perhaps have an agreement or plan in place before you start.

People that work for you will make mistakes and most of them will care about it. Remember, you are not perfect and think about what you can do to make the next mistake less painful for everybody. Try to show appreciation and say something positive about their attitude or work rate etc. Keep things real and do not be afraid to spell things out. Naturally, keep questions open and try not to create an atmosphere of interrogation. Always think about how you would have done things. Remember the possibility that they do not have your experience or perhaps all the information you do. Do all this privately. Remember, reward publicly and reprimand privately. When the business has gone through difficult periods, my sister has always been the most positive person around and she keeps me grounded. For me, she is a legend.

The idea of 'my door is always open' is something that you need to commit to and practice rather than it be a figure of speech.

Chapter Fourteen
Fear the Perfectionist

This, for me, is an interesting one and probably one of my more controversial opinions.

How often have you heard someone say, "The problem is, I am a bit of a perfectionist," and they say it with pride. In my book (and this is my book), this is nothing to be proud of, but something to be really wary of. With your business, there is a need to get things right and a requirement in all companies to have people that care but perfectionism brings its own challenges.

Why is a perfectionist a problem for business? A company's functions are about time and money. If you are given plenty of money to do a task, then you can take your time with it. But if money is tight, then the chances are you need to provide your solution quicker for you to make money. Quite simply, you can do anything with enough time and money.

A true perfectionist will never quite be satisfied that the task is complete, which suggests, regardless of the time you give them, they will fill it and the challenge is that they will never quite finish. As a budding businessperson, you will know that you are in the business of selling time and making money.

Let me give you some clarity. If you own a window cleaning company, you are selling a service. It takes you an hour to do each house, so that time has a value if a customer pays £20 to have their windows cleaned. If you can do two houses in an hour rather than one and can still maintain your service levels, you make twice the money, same vehicles, people, training, branding and marketing. A perfectionist will focus on results and that is good, but the result might be unrealistic because of the time it takes to complete! The window cleaner will probably never complete more than one house in an hour and there is a danger they may even take longer. If you link this to someone who is highly critical, you end up with someone worrying about things and never getting the job finished because nothing is quite good enough and this, in turn, will also stop you making money.

So how much time do we invest? How do we work out the rate? And how do we work out what the acceptable standard is for the product?

What you are always trying to do is add value and create perceived value. That all sounds like business bull, so let me explain this as well. Let us go back to basics. In sales, we are taught the real basics of 'features', 'benefits' and 'you appeal' when we are trying to make a sale. The terminology changes over time as fashion and trends drive the words but the meanings stay the same. If that doesn't make sense, maybe this will help. You are a salesman, trying to sell chairs to an office manager, who has an issue with the stability of their current chairs. Your chair has five legs, this is the tangible aspect about the chair and so is a feature. You then work on what benefit the five legs has for the buyer that it makes the chair rock solid and connects perfectly with the floor when you use it. This is the 'benefit'. The 'you appeal' has to be tailored to your customer and the person buying the goods. The five legs mean that when you sit on it, you will not fall off and hurt yourself. So you are not selling the five legs to the customer, you are selling the stability of the chairs and the solution this provides.

The challenge with the perfectionist is, they will have a strong focus on all the features and benefits and may not link specific features and benefits, the 'you appeal' to the customer! Other factors also get involved in the sales process. A perfectionist is similar in some ways to a high achiever, in that, the goals are set very high. However, a high achiever will get as good as they can and then be satisfied with how well they have done. They will try to improve again next time, but not worry about the performance for long because they will have another go later. A perfectionist will never be quite satisfied and the job will never be quite finished, 'almost perfect' will be seen as a failure. A person who is a perfectionist is very self-critical and pushed by fear, so might not actually be content with the results. To stop the fear setting in, they tend to procrastinate. This will affect productivity and the delays and perceived failure will make the person defensive. It is unhealthy if this develops into the person thinking they are a failure and not good enough.

There are some good traits in a person who wants their work to be absolutely correct. The standards they set are high and they always aim to exceed expectations. We all want to provide a product that is better than the customer asked for but managing that and pitching the product/service correctly means the client will feel they are getting value for money and not a bargain. If a customer feels they are getting a bargain, then the price is not high enough, so you need to increase prices and make more money! Remember, that is why you are here!

I would suggest that we all strive for excellence. We all try to be better and we measure our progress. If we can enjoy the result and smile when a customer is happy, then we are in the place we need to be.

As a manufacturer and as a business with no major start up investment, I had to develop the product as I went along. Some solutions were better than others but I always worked on continuous improvement to ensure the next product was better than the last. I am proud that customers visit our show booths asking what the latest updates are. I am not sure if I would have got this far if I was a perfectionist, in fact, I am sure I would not have.

Being a perfectionist is not a behaviour, it is a way of thinking. Your role as the boss is to set a standard of work that the customer is happy to pay for. As your standards and quality increase, so can the product value and the prices. If your profit is a constant percentage of what you do, then with a little luck, you will make more profit.

Sounds easy!

Chapter Fifteen
Don't Boil the Water, Fix the Leak

This title does not, lie but as with everything, it is never that simple to avoid. Taking the correct action is something completely different. As you have guessed this is the same as 'throwing the baby out with the bath water'.

When you start delegating to a small team, you will, without really knowing it, start introducing different levels of trust and start relying on others to do their work unsupervised. If you want to grow the business, you have to but this takes a while to get used to. From time to time things will go wrong and some of these will be 'major cockups'.

Interestingly, in my experience, the 'major cock ups' are easier to manage because, usually, everyone knows what the problem is and that it needs to be fixed. Sometimes, you will see things you are not happy with. Some will feel it is OK and acceptable while others may have missed the error completely. The latter is more of a challenge because it suggests a problem with the standards you have created or a process you have implemented that has not concluded in the result you wanted. This must be challenged. You need to investigate and work out if the process is wrong or has not been followed. It could be down to people either needing training or lacking ability (remember chapter eight 'right person right box'). It can also be that some are just lazy or do not care. You will have to deal with that and (god help you) performance manage them out of the business over time unless you spot them early! Most processes involve several people and departments, so it could be a failure in communication. Either way, it needs to be resolved to stop the error being repeating. If you are a good people person, you can read situations and gain trust and over time, you can develop both a good business ethos and various levels of personal relationships within the company.

There is a time and place for corrective instruction, training and development and there are dozens of books on different management styles. Everyone learns in a different way, so when correcting someone, you need to keep everything in context and assess how the person receiving your 'corrective instruction' responds and learns from it.

I remember a skipper friend of mine talking to a member of my staff on a sailing team building day in the Solent. I was the designated tea boy, keeping my team fed and watered and Jimbo was skipper, making sure everyone got something out of the day. The team were getting to grips with their roles, starting to speed up and grow in confidence. They were also starting to get a bit cheeky when one of them made an error and looked up and apologised, "Sorry, Jimbo," he said.

Well, Jimbo just looked at him, smiled and in the most sarcastic manor said, "I don't want you to be sorry. I want you to be better!" It completely cracked everyone up. Now, of course, in a real situation, you cannot word things that way, but on that day, it was perfect. The team loved it and believe me, despite it being a fun day, none of them wanted to be told to be 'better'. The tone reminded them that the day was fun, not formal but you have to love a little peer pressure because everyone tried just a little harder after that. Ever since that day, I have been looking for an opportunity to use that line but not managed it yet!

More seriously, never shoot from the hip or make a rash decision or statement. As a business owner, you usually have to make big decisions, and, of course, you will get used to doing this quickly, but my top tip is always take a deep breath, get a cuppa and take a moment before you go off all guns blazing. Try to take the emotion out of your approach. I have often written a strong email just to get something off my chest but have not sent it just rewritten it.

I have often seen things happen in my business that I am not happy with. It is so easy to make a snap judgement. Anyone can do that, so it is important to not only keep everything in context but also get a true picture of the problem. I only see some of the team for short snippets of time and it always amazes me that the impression I am given is not the same as that of the line manager, who manages that team and sees their overall performance. So be patient and count to ten. Not always easy, I know.

I will give you an example of a real situation where I could have completely lost it. One of our vehicles is a high-top Luton van. It is just about the biggest thing you can drive with a standard car licence being around 3m high. it is used by our fitters when doing installations around the country. On this occasion, our guys arrived on site to refit the CCTV control room in a shopping centre and were directed to drive the van through a barrier and down into the basement car park.

The driver did not check the height clearance of the basement and proceeded to take the top half-metre of the van off as he hit the roof of the car park! I then get a call from the driver but not before he posted a photo of the incident on Facebook, which someone made me aware of. Not only had he breached our social media policy but he proceeded to reject the fact he was to blame, telling me it was the customers fault because he was told where to park and directed to the underground area.

There is no process or instruction within our employee handbook on how to make sure you do not hit anything. There is nothing telling you to ignore the customer because he might be wrong but there is a section about your responsibilities and duty of care! As you can imagine, I was ready to completely freak out. Was this gross misconduct? Meaning, he could be fired or was it just an accident? Did he care about the incident or was he lazy not paying attention and not bothered? Well, I took a breath, had a cuppa and decided to talk to him on his return the next day after having the photo removed from social media. After a short conversation with his line manager, I find out the guy is usually of good character, reliable and trustworthy. He does have a bit of an attitude and he does tend to get defensive when he has made a mistake. To be honest, before this conversation, I was ready to let him go. I talked to the customer, of course, he was not going to take any of the blame, whatsoever, but he did tell us not to worry about the roof we hit! Apparently, we were not the first and we would not be asked to make or pay for any repairs. When the guys returned from site, we followed a set process and investigated the cause of the collision, reminding the drivers of the height of the vehicle as stated in the cab. The driver, to be fair, did accept responsibility and is still with us today. We just don't let him drive the van!

As you may know by now, I am not a fan of processes, but they really do help and over time, I have gone from thinking they are simply slowing the business down to being vital in that everyone knows what is expected. If you treat people correctly, they usually respond and others looking in will see that. I have become a bit of a process policeman.

There is a line between making quick and possibly rash decisions that could see you boiling the water rather than fixing the kettle and doing the opposite, which is to over analyse every decision.

I would suggest the main thing to consider here is the difference between a quick decision and a rash one. If the quick one does not have a great impact, then just do it. Measure the risk and decide how much time the decision warrants. This is very important when it involves people because there will be more emotion involved.

As companies grow, the processes usually develop with it, but a tip here is to keep decision processes in check. Some decisions are so small and non-critical that an educated gamble can be made. The best example I have was the purchase of an edge banding machine we were talking about acquiring in order to speed up a production process. We had just gone through a major machinery investment that I had decided was important to the future proofing of the product. It was largely driven by me with not all the managers as committed. We worked hard calculating the return-on-investment period and met several times about it. Including a government investment grant the complete project cost over £200k. This was the largest single investment we had ever made and it was this that, perhaps, had an effect on the edge banding machine purchase, where we had completely got lost in the process. The new machine was less than £1,000, although it was worth some investigation, a bit of internet research maybe to ensure we were purchasing the right machine. It was not worthy of valuable management time. Larger companies would have a cost to risk method to decide what decision-making path was taken but we were not and are still not there yet.

Chapter Sixteen
Do Not Forget to Smell the Roses

This is an expression a business partner used after work one Friday. In the early days of the company, when there were only three or four people employed, every few weeks in the summer we would nip to the local pub for a pint before going home.

I guess this was two or more years in and the company was finally starting to show some stability. The stress levels had started to drop a little because there were signs of traction and regular work. The phone was starting to ring with people wanting the product. I have to say it is a fantastic feeling when your potential customers start calling you!

We finished one Friday and all of us went to the local Pub, the Fishers Pond. We grabbed a pint and walked out to the back of the building, where there was of course a large pond, hence the name. The sun was shining and Paul turned to me and said, "It's time to stop and smell the roses!" Not a flower in sight but it was five minutes to just pause and realise that we had a good week.

Do not think for one second I did not have 50 things I could be worrying about but the point is, when you have a good day, week or month, make the most of that moment. It is vital you celebrate the wins and also as important to keep the tough moments in perspective. Paul was right, so when we get the opportunity, we celebrate, either in a small way with something small like a drink on the way home or something bigger, such as a family day for the company or a cash bonus.

We also introduced employee of the month, celebrating individual achievements, where someone has gone 'over and above' in their work or where what they have achieved has really helped another person or team within the business. The employee of the month gets the best parking spot at the front of the building and a shopping voucher and in return, the company take a photo, put it on the wall and post it on social media. We all get a little something out of it and I have always been surprised how people like the prime parking spot. It does provide a bit of kudos. I once had to stop someone trying to auction it off one month because it had value!

When we celebrate, we always work on the personal touch regardless of whether it is an individual, a team or the entire company. All employees on reaching ten years' service receive a cut glass crystal award and we hold a company meeting celebrating their highlights and journey within the business.

People may leave a company if they feel undervalued and some management feel a reward could introduce complacency that has never been the case in my experience.

Celebrating well can bring a feeling of inclusion and it will help the bonding and team spirit within the company. It does need to feel special though, so do make sure the joy is proportional to the win. Try to make the celebration a note of appreciation. I do this by saying a few words about the achievement.

But, this is not all about the employees. You must remember to step back and look at your achievements, however small. Some of the things you did in the early days now seem so insignificant but at the time it was like climbing a mountain. I remember opening my first business bank account. I thought this would be simple but I had to provide a lot of information on the application form and needed to provide identification. I did not have a business address at the time which made it challenging. I have celebrated quite a few firsts. A big one for me was when I saw a project finished on the production floor that I was not involved with. I still remember seeing the project with surprise. I opened a nice bottle of red that night because for the first time, things were happening without any of my personal involvement. It was a milestone in our growth. Today, I try to remind myself how lucky I am to have choices. My team have to come to work to get paid. I get paid regardless. During the COVID pandemic, I was asked several times if jobs were safe. I was able to re-assure people because we had cash reserves and forward sales. It put me in a privileged position and even if that is not a celebration, then it is a consequence of success and something I could be grateful for.

Professional companies find it hard to celebrate success because growth and money are the reward we should ask ourselves what success looks like. I remember when I took my first proper holiday after starting the company, for me, that was a big positive. For others, it will securing a big order, money in the bank, employing more staff but what if the managers are now getting more leisure time! Is that a win? My top tip is to tie your goals in with the aims and culture of the business. They do not have to all be about performance, growth and profit. If we only focus on the mechanics of success, we might not enjoy the journey and time is one thing you cannot get back. Perhaps success is much more a process rather than a finishing line.

As an owner, there is a need to be optimistic and to take pride in what you do. I always wanted to build the best products we could and make profit doing so. I also share stories and try to take pride in what is being created. It is not the biggest, richest, fastest growing or most fantastic company in the world, but I am proud of the people that work for me and where we are. Remember, to reward yourself, very rarely will you be told you are good at what you do because it is your job to tell others.

One of my proudest work moments was not when we won a couple of national awards, but when we celebrated our first 15 years. The team presented me with various gifts marking this milestone I was really touched. The icing on the cake was when the managers pulled me into a meeting and presented me with some cufflinks – a set that had the company start date, the 15-year date and the latitude and longitude coordinates of the first office. A nice personal link to my love of sailing and just a really lovely thing to do.

I guess the final word on this is a mental one. Everybody uses different coping mechanisms and running a business is tough. Celebrating the wins is so important because everyone can see that things are going well, it can be like opening a pressure valve of stress when something good happens, so make sure that you notice these when they occur. In business, you are always short of something, either materials, labour or orders and if you can get used to this and manage it, then you are developing. Not sweating the small stuff and coping with unknowns should also be celebrated in some way. It could be as small a gesture as making the tea or bringing in the biscuits.

There is also evidence that success breeds success. It can grow confidence and a positive mind set. That is as good a reason as any to always remember to 'stop and smell the roses'.

Chapter Seventeen
Cut Once and Cut Deep

I wish I could just talk to you about how my companies grew without any problems, but that is not the reality. I experienced many bumps along the road and a lot of the time they were caused by things that I had no control over. This chapter is not about the good times. It is about the tough periods, how to spot them early, how to manage them and what to do about them and to do this, we are going to focus on the impact recession can have on your business.

If the economy slows or shrinks, then it hits most businesses. I would suggest that you need to have a business growth of 5% a year just to say you are standing still. For the first five years, a new business should expect a much higher growth, your motivation is at its peak, the product or service will be fresh and will at least have an angle to attack each market from and providing you have done your homework, you know there is a need or demand for what you are offering. The growth we experienced not including the first five years has been around 10%, so steady rather than spectacular.

The first recession I experienced was in 2008. I had been trading for five years and was into the second year of a lease for a workshop too big for me! Moving into the new property emptied the reserves of cash. Never underestimate the cost to physically move your business as I did. For the first couple of months I was sort of in denial and I did not see the signs. We had a lot of quotes; the sales guys were relatively busy but the win rate had dropped and everything started to take longer to get over the line and converted into business. One thing for sure in the UK is we can talk ourselves into a recession!

It is hard as an owner not to have any emotion in your company. I would suggest that some of the best businesspeople I know have been able to remove this attachment and have more clarity. This does have negatives as well as positives, but when things are looking 'not so rosy', clarity is required.

The mission is to protect the money you have and not lose too much. You need to focus on this 100% at the first sign of things dipping. In hindsight we could see it coming but our reputation and personal pride probably slowed the management reaction time. Try to be aware of this as it is even more difficult when the decisions you make affect people around you. I deeply care about the people who work for me and their view of the business. Every day I try to make sure we look after the people here as much as we can. The challenge comes when you must start making savings. This will inevitably include reducing the salary bill. When things are contracting, it is time to be ruthless and put the numbers first. The saving grace is you do get the opportunity to get rid of anyone who no longer fits the business. Remember as a company grows, a person that was perfect when there was only three of you may no longer be right when there are 30 of you. A business always needs a good mix of people with different skills and if we get the planning and balance of people correct and continue our assessment of what the business needs and what we must do to provide for it, you will feel the performance benefits.

A company is always short of one of the following, customers, product to sell or people to do the work. When we have lots of material, lots of staff and not enough business, then we must make changes. Although salaries are usually one of the largest costs to a business, this might not be the only area for cutbacks, so you need to create a plan. What will the business look like next month or in two or three years' time and post-recession? Who will we need where and how can we get the growth started again without running out of money during the journey?

When it comes to cutting your team, be as objective as you can and try and remove the emotion, not easy, I know. Honesty is the best policy. Tell the team you must reduce the number of people and that you are personally working on it. This is not the time to hide away but a time to step up. Follow your processes, everyone who is at threat of losing their job should be told as soon as possible. The chances are you will have a lack of work longer than you realise. This means you must cut DEEP. As the title suggests, try to reduce as much as you can, you will only want to do this ONCE because the experience is not great for anyone involved, so work hard to cut ONCE and cut DEEP.

Be aware that this is one of the hardest things you will have to do but if you do not, it could possibly take down the whole company. Remember, you are making someone redundant, that does not make them or you a bad person. Even when you are not in a recession and you need to let someone go because of performance or changes to the business, do it as quickly, cleanly and kindly as you can. Blame the situation, blame the economy or tell them that perhaps they are not right for the business at this time, be as truthful as you can be. This is a gentle way of taking the blame away from the person you are letting go.

The very first time I had to fire someone, happened a good ten years before I started my own company. A regional sales guy was way down on his numbers which I first thought was due to a looming recession. Being based 200 miles away, made managing him quite difficult. I had attended customer visits with him the previous year. He was always great in front of clients. His reports were all positive and everything I could see did not suggest any issues. All the other areas of the business not related to his patch were OK and I could not work out what was wrong. Each salesperson in my team had a quote target, a visit target, cold call target, and new business target. My man was hitting all these numbers.

I was stumped, so I called a mate of mine for his advice, and over a pint we talked about the rep and his approach, his quotes, his area, his clients, his personality and I could not see the problem. We worked out that there was only one more thing to do. I got on the phone and called all the people he had met over the last two months. The response from the first three calls gave me my answer. "Yes, your man is always great on the end of the phone when we need him."

"Hang on!" I said. "According to our records, he visited you twice in the last six weeks and has quoted three projects." The phone went quiet for a few seconds. The customer double checked we were talking about the same person, then confirmed he had not had any contact with him for six months or so and had not asked for any quotes in that time either. I found that quite confusing because I had received a quarterly travel summary that showed he had been visited three times! I also had a quotation report that detailed two projects!

It turned out that my man was setting up one meeting a day, driving to the meeting in order to claim the fuel and register the mileage on the car, then driving directly home. Because he was 'in meetings' and 'driving', he could not be contacted either. It turned out later, he was renovating a property. I was shocked and quite angry to begin with, then did something I have got better at over time. I sat on this information and gave myself time to reflect and work out a plan.

This meant another pint with my friend to go over everything and he came out with a cracking line, "Get him down to your office, look him in the eye and tell him it is not often you get the opportunity to mix business with pleasure, but you can today, you're bloody fired." Of course, I did not and could not say that, but the line stuck with me for a few years!

Anyway, the sales guy came down to the office and we followed the gross misconduct process that included a couple of hearings and an opportunity for him to explain himself. The process was set out in the employee manual, so we followed that to the letter and he was out of a job within three days. For me, trust is everything, especially with remote workers.

What was interesting was after the event, I felt a massive release. I had not slept for days. When I told him, his expression did not change. I am sure he knew he was losing his job before he arrived at the office.

On another occasion I had to lose a member of the team I liked. She had done absolutely nothing wrong making the decision much more difficult. I did all I could to remind her that it was not her I was making redundant but her role within the business. We paid her notice period and allowed her to leave right away because she was quite upset.

On another occasion I had to let a young guy go because of a downturn, who again was a really nice person. He chose to work his notice and when he left, he came into my office and thanked me for the years of training and faith I had put in him. You just cannot judge how people will react.

I learnt a lot from a former boss about how to handle people. She was a fantastic people person and I hope I have managed to retain some of things she taught me. We had to give a member of staff a written warning over time keeping. They were young, living at home and enjoying life. Late nights did not always mean they would make work the next morning. Helen and I sat them down and reminded them about the company policies. The things they should have done. We showed them the full history of their attendance record and how many chances we had given them until that meeting. Halfway through me talking, they started to cry. Helen, who sat next to me, raised her hand , leaned forward and instructed the employee to excuse themselves, go to the washroom and pull themselves together, then return so we could continue the meeting. I was, wow, that is strong, but they did it. Within 30 seconds, they were back! It was a complete act to try and get my sympathy. Lucky for me, Helen had seen it all before, it was a real eye opener for me. We finished the meeting and got back to work. The member of staff was fine and in fact the meeting had the desired affect and they stayed with us for a number of years.

It was a great learning moment for me and I hope now also for you. Keep it formal, keep it professional and give someone time out if they need to get it together.

The second recession we experienced came much faster and harder but was expected. I am talking about the Corona Pandemic (COVID-19). This was managed in a different way. We did, however, have some choices as we had access to government support and were able to furlough people. Unfortunately, we still had to make some redundancies. The big positive for me was after being in business for over 18 years. I had built in reserves to get us through a recession, the downside was having to lose some very good people. When times are tough, you do really find out who your friends are. I try not to hold a grudge but from experience, these won't be your corporate landlords or banks.

It is not just about cutting staff in a downturn. My advice would be to plan as well as you can and to reduce both marketing and IT as late as possible. Those parts of the business could pay for themselves later. For me, the challenge was slowing down major project investments. During COVID-19, we were mid-way through a very expensive software upgrade. We had also committed to several software licences we could not get out of, exposing us to high cost. So everyone kept their cars for another year, salary reviews were put on hold and we talked to our suppliers about slowing deliveries as they were in the same situation as us. Remember to keep your lines of communication open as much as you can, not just with suppliers but with your internal people.

Chapter Eighteen
Cash is King

When I started my very first company, this was the soundest advice I was given and by carrying this throughout my career, it has kept us solvent and helped me sleep at night. It is something I completely believe in and highly recommend new businesses to remember 'Cash is King'.

This is not brown paper bags full of £20 notes. This is about the flow of money through the business. Accountants call it cash flow and quite simply put, you need to get it coming in before it goes out.

The starting point in your head must be completely selfish. In that, your need is greater than theirs. It still amazes me that every company we deal with instantly expects credit terms of usually 30 days from the date we delivered the goods. What you are doing is trusting someone to pay you for goods they received a month ago. My first question to you is, where is their motivation to pay you promptly on time? They already have the goods, so what do they care. You must bear this in mind, in the early days, there were a few ways to calculate the risk of not getting paid. Now nearly 20 years later, the world of credit scoring is only a click away, so there are definitely no excuses not to check the risk. This, however, does not guarantee prompt payment, so my starting position on any project is not to give credit terms.

There are some really basic fundamentals here that you have to understand. Now I am definitely not an accountant and I am going to assume you are not either but this is important to remember. If you lend anyone money i.e. give credit, then you are losing money and exposing yourself to risk (unless you charge for it). As a company, you can still go under if you do not have good cash flow, even if you have a massive forward order book with a profitable business. Believe me, I have seen it.

When you have a new business, it is difficult. A high percentage of start-up businesses do not survive their first year and a lot of this is down to cash flow. Their start-up money runs out before their product or service was paid for or enough demand created. There are several ways to protect yourself as much as you can from cash flow issues and you must use them all as much as you can. Here are a few methods we have used in the past. Everything in this book, as you know, relates to true experiences, so all these things have worked for me at different times.

To start, see if you can pass down the terms and conditions from your client to your suppliers. This is never easy if your business is quite new. Getting long term credit from suppliers might not be viable but if your new business is with a Blue-chip client, sometimes a supplier will accept the same payment terms if you explain the situation. If they want 90 days payment, ask the same of your material supplier.

In my first year, I won a big order with a local authority to fit out their control room. UK British government departments have an obligation to pay on time but as with most local authorities, the admin process is often slow and can delay things. On the plus side, chances are you will get paid (eventually). As soon as I received an order, I sent an invoice. A nice lady rang me within five minutes asking me what I was doing. I simply said as a new account and under the terms of our trading conditions, all new accounts must pay up front as they have no credit history with us. It took a few phone calls and I was on the charm offensive for a couple of days but a week later, I was paid in full for the job I had not yet started.

Another suggestion is to plan the cash flow, which so many start-ups seem to miss. For the first 18 months, I did not pay myself, every penny stayed within the business to fund the projects. The company sold products that started at £5k, so if I won two or three in the same month, I could not fund them. To make it work, I planned and managed each quarter and I always tried to keep cash in the bank. I would always push for orders and would never defer something to the following month to make numbers look good. This is called sandbagging which I cover later in the book. This meant I could look at the sales numbers and work out what my cash flow was going to look like, depending on the terms given. There is just no excuse for this now, because mobile apps and online banks do this for you instantly. I am amazed by the bank resources that are now available for my children to use that help them manage their money each month.

The next tip is to send the invoice right away. Get the payment demand on the customers system. This is not boring admin and not something you should leave for later. I have seen companies forget to invoice customers altogether.

Also remember that you can lease rather than buy. Cars and machinery can all be leased when necessary and if it helps cash flow. I remember when I had been going around eight years, a bank offered us a lease deal on a vehicle. They could not understand why I would want to own one. The answer was simple, owning the car made me more money as leasing a car has a cost involved. The bank manager said I should lease to create cash flow but we had plenty of cash. We were eight years in and had money in the bank, so by paying cash, we saved on interest rate costs and set up fees, therefore, making us more money.

If you get asked for payment terms, start with staged payments, particularly if there is a long production time. Introducing payment milestones can really help. If you are providing a service, you could bring in a service agreement or payment loan.

From day one, I looked for ways to help my cash flow and the main solution came when I started TSS Engineering. The business model was much lower value, parts sales and repeat business. What it gave us was cash flow by way of small orders placed regularly and repeatedly.

Try to manage your own expectations and pick your battles with the customers you want to work with, especially in the early days. For the first few years, I really wanted to work with local authorities because I knew they would not go bust and they usually pay on time. It would have been great to work with some big private firms but the risk at the start was too high.

Interestingly, what does change things is if you manage to create demand for your product/service. This is probably one of the hardest things to do and tough for a start-up. Let us imagine you have a new super recipe for your baked beans, they suddenly become very popular with customers. This then puts you in the driving seat with the supermarket and gives you more negotiating power. The supermarket wants to sell your beans as it will bring in more customers. You can now agree a better price for your beans or agree better terms, all of which will help to increase your cash flow.

Some other simple ways to keep cash flow positive include making sure you keep your stock levels low or at least managed. In addition, work on your costs regularly, everything from material costs down to rent, insurance and utility bills. They all affect cash flow. Keep in contact with your accountant, often they will not charge for this sort of advice and they might spot line items in your accounts that look too high for you to investigate. Keep a forecast of cash moving forward and try to plan. Try to anticipate problems. I do consider banks as fair-weather friends but keep them informed and up to date. You will always find them more approachable before something happens rather than when it is too late. Remove any excuses by your client to delay payment. Get the product and service right and when you send the invoice, make sure the documentation is perfect. The values match the quote, the dates are correct, the distribution is accurate and you have sent it to the correct person.

Non-profitable businesses can continue for a while with good cash flow but profitable businesses can fold if they do not have good cash management.

Chapter Nineteen
Hunt the Truth

This chapter is about you being the Boss and the pitfalls around being regarded as the top dog.

I have always tried to create a no blame culture within the business and I suggest you do this as well. Work at creating an environment where we are learning and developing together. It means nothing to some people but to others, it will have a good positive effect.

You need to be acutely aware that to some people you are not 'Wayne, the fitter', who started a business in his dining room, but the grey-haired bloke charging around in a hurry. Some staff will only know you as the person in charge, and because of our personality alone, employees are going to be careful. It is in my nature and in that of a lot of company owners, not to deviate from the task, which makes us quite direct and perhaps sometimes a bit aggressive. We do not even realise we are because in our heads, we are just trying to get things done. Let me put this another way. I am focused and do not have time for grey areas. For me, it is black or white. The challenge is, there are quite a lot of grey areas in life and if you are not aware of this, you can miss out on important facts and details that you need to know about.

Hunting the truth is problem solving. It is about finding out what is not working because some of your team will not want to tell you what is actually wrong. People generally do not mean to make mistakes and do not want to highlight them or confess. This is why there should be a drive and commitment to openness. In addition, they do not want to tell their boss they are wrong (even if they are) because they also think they are usually right! This can also be made more difficult if the business has been successful. The boss will take the credit for success and that will breed confidence but it might also bring some arrogance. You have to hunt the truth, get the answers you need and be as open as you can.

The success of the business might not be down to you? I must also add here the failure of the business might not be down to you either.

'You have two ears and one mouth. Use them in that ratio' is quite an old line but is true. Another is, 'Don't throw the baby out with the bath water'. These are all about getting all the information before you act. You have to try and find out what the real problem is before you attempt to fix it. We have already talked about this but what I am talking about here is more about you as a person.

As an example, I want to talk about my business partner who is one of the kindest nicest men I have had the pleasure of working with. Paul A, is really well-read and studies business like an expert studying the inner workings of a classic wristwatch. He often observes things and then comes to me for a chat. Now Paul is a director. He does not need to run things by me. He has full authority to do what he wants, so why is he sat here with me? The truth is, he is trying to improve me! That is not easy but he is right. I know I am not perfect so I should always strive to develop my own skills to improve and so should you.

Hunting the truth might result in you needing to hear some home truths about yourself. As an entrepreneur, you have a certain type of personality which might not be easy to approach. Work hard to surround yourself with people like Paul that are happy to come to you and speak honestly.

Some of the best advice I have had has not come from business coaches or advisers, who I pay but by other owners and managers who quite frankly could not care less if I ignored them.

By their nature, entrepreneurs are not charismatic. God, I try to be every day, but it is a smoke screen. As you develop your management skills, you also start learning from experiences, which is where you get wisdom from. It certainly does not come from age alone. Using this experience and responsibility can only help you grow as a person. Sometimes, we become more impatient and complain more. That is because we have experienced good things and want that more often. It is a challenge to be patient but it is worthwhile. It is good for business if you are a happy person.

As the boss, you tend to have a few 'YES' men around. I use the word figuratively as it can be a women. I want to be questioned and you should desire this too. It is how we check and justify what we do. A lot of the time some clarification and explanation is all that is needed and to be honest it can be even better when people are fully on board.

There are a few odd quirks that go with running a business. Managing people is one of the biggest challenges and there are a lot of books on the subject. I knew at the start when I was writing my plan that I had to employ people. As a manufacturing company, it is sort of inevitable. What you are never taught is how to be a boss or an employer. Being an entrepreneur is a lonely game. You have to have self-belief, bloody mindedness and a fire in your belly. Personally, I am the complete cliché when it comes to the entrepreneur/business owner. Driving things all the time, bored easily, never contented, believe me these are not perfect attributes to have all the time.

The 'boss' thing is weird to get used to and I will never forget when I overheard a couple of the guys talking in the workshop and referring to me as the 'old man'. I was completely gutted!

As your company grows, you will need to put effort into processes and people. My experience so far and a good thing to know is that generally people want to know the rules of the game. What is expected of them? How they should act at work and have a clear understanding of what good looks like? It is tough when you realise that just because it is not your way, it is not necessary the wrong way. Unless you delegate, you will never really grow and if you do not trust, you will never switch off.

I have chatted to a lot of business owners about this. One of my skills is to be able to give responsibility and to look after people. It is all very selfish, really. I want people to like me and to achieve that I try to give them all I can and to make them feel involved. My company has a culture committee and offers a family day, development and training plans, free fruit etc. We are not one of these high-flying city companies with slides and pool tables but we try.

I am constantly trying to make the business a nicer place to work. As I do so it attracts better people and part of my plan is to have better people involved. Sometimes, I can be quite a miserable sod but that is because I am the one who has to push for perfect and remind everyone what good looks like. Generally, the more you pay, the higher the skill set of people you attract. Quite straight forward really, there is some method to my madness and if you put this beside the fact I am quite lazy, then empowering people is definitely required.

To better the business, you do need to speak to people. You will probably not get the truth when in a group, so work on getting team members in a one to one. I have learnt more with an employee over a pint or a drink in a coffee shop, than when sat in my office. When you are together, try not to get a round of questions going but work on moving the conversation around and get engagement. One of my old bosses used to say that silence is a conversation. Quite often a silent period is filled with a truth, so be patient and let the other person talk. They may not have much to say but this one to one gives them the opportunity to open up and if they do, then show that you are listening by nodding. I often summarise to make sure I have understood and I never try to look surprised or let the person think it is a massive deal. You need to keep any questions open but that is a given and I have often told someone a worse story or example just to keep things in balance. You need to avoid being defensive or aggressive if you are told something unexpected. Show empathy where needed and do all you can to understand. Another thing I try to do is let the person know they are not alone in telling you something.

Remember, you are hunting the truth, so it might not be there right away.

Chapter Twenty
Small Steps Across the Atlantic

Setting up, developing and running a business is a journey. It can take a long time to grow or can take off very quickly but either way there are various stages or steps the growth goes through.

I have stressed earlier in this book the need to have a plan but, hey, we don't have a crystal ball so be prepared to change the plan. When I started, I wrote a plan and kept a copy in my desk. With a complete lack of knowledge and experience, my plan was to be turning over a million pounds within five years and five million within ten years. For the record, I achieved the five-year target but it took an additional 15 years to grow to five million (an explanation why will be in the next book). I was way out and even further out if you look at the steps I planned. For me, measuring and creating small steps is so important in the development of a company. It checks your progress and checks your sanity because small steps help you see the progress you are making. Am I doing the right thing? Is this getting me closer to my aim? These are the questions I constantly ask myself.

What does the destination look like? This is goal setting, which is something that you will need to do sometimes, working on a big project such as growing a company can be daunting and a slog, not just for you but for everyone in the business and everyone around you. One way to cope is to remember to 'smell the roses' but another way is to focus on 'small gains' or 'small steps. For one year, my management team had a monthly meeting agenda that started with 'making gains' as the opening headline. It was about asking ourselves what we have achieved, what have we gained and how can we make more gains next month. It is a useful management tool to understand when to look at the journey of a business in both small steps and longer-term journeys, knowing when to apply each can really help your perspective.

When the firm is hit by a recession, a key employee leaves or you lose a big client, the performance and moral of the business is affected. To keep yourself positive and to motivate others during periods like this becomes harder because by looking at things in small chunks, the big single event has overshadowed it. It is at these moments you need to consider the future plan and the bigger picture. If, for example, a key department manager decides to leave you, there is going to be some short-term pain in recruiting and training someone new. These are the next few small steps but what the ex-employee will not do is affect the long-term plan. It might delay things or perhaps it could actually speed things up and push you on (for example if you employ the right person). The objective here is to know what you are looking at, is it a step or a leap. As a leader, you are there to pull out the positives and the experience from the event, so you can learn and develop not just yourself but the remaining people. We can all see the bad news but you will be surprised how resourceful you can be when you need to give people something positive to work with.

One mistake I made in the early days, which I mentioned earlier in the book, was the reverse of this situation. A local competitor went bust giving us a quick increase in growth. We took some of their team and won some of their clients, I took the small step approach. Looking back, perhaps, I should have been more confident and taken most of their staff, their workshop and their client base. This would have accelerated my plan. Small steps can work both ways.

I have a couple more personal examples that so easily link back to the business I want to share with you.

During a family holiday in Normandy, we were sat on a beach and around 100 yards out was a concrete dive platform. When we arrived, the tide was out and my children who I guess were around 8 and 12 years old at the time were able to run out and play on it. As the day went on and the tide started to come in, I called them back to the beach as I did not want them stuck. They did this but then of course decided later to swim out to it when the tide was much further in. Some larger kids were now diving off the platform and having a great time. What I did not notice was a little girl stood on the platform quite scared and not diving! I then recognised her this was my Katie and Dad had to swim out to her and get her back.

She was not happy. She was scared and a little cold sat on this platform while bigger kids were having a great time jumping in and out of the sea. There was no real danger other than, perhaps, her getting a little too cold. After some coaxing and encouragement, it was quite clear that Dad knew nothing and she was not going to try to swim back to the beach because it now looked miles away with the tide fully in. So I'm sat there with her working out plan 'B'.

Plan 'B' turned out to me changing my tact from gentle Dad to 'suck it up and start bloody swimming, Dad!' I jumped in the water and got her in and we started swimming. Katie is a great swimmer, but it was a long way to the beach. I stayed beside her as we slowly made for shore. After five minutes of effort, the beach still looked very far away and the perception was little or no progress and Katie was starting to worry. There was no way I could carry her. She had to keep swimming. I then remembered the small steps, gave her a hug and re-assured her and held her for a few seconds so she could catch her breath. I turned her around to show her how far we had come because although the beach looked a long way away, so now did the platform. We had made progress for sure. I re-assured her that all was fine. I showed her the small steps of progress and told her we need to crack on and she did. I talked her into an agreement that we would stop two more times and off we went. We stopped again after another five minutes and then finally, we were touching the bottom and walking up the beach. When we got to our group, we did not celebrate or make a deal out of it. We just said we swam back together. It was a moment of achievement and a small gain, rather than a big celebration.

Linking this to work can be done on many levels. Your approach to problems is important but being able to change it and perhaps break larger challenges down to smaller manageable ones is a good idea. Staying positive and reassuring your team is of course used everywhere but also having a break and cutting someone some slack is important. Equally giving someone a hug along the way helps (perhaps more metaphorically). Being in it together as a team is important, especially during moments that are quite stressful. However, there are times when you need to be the boss and times when not to make a big deal out of things.

When you go through a single year of a business, you have goals, milestones and objectives but they always must be kept in context. If you then try to forecast a five-year plan or longer, you must make some big assumptions, so don't worry if they don't work out, change the plan (try plan 'B').

Example number two is a bit grander.

I got into sailing in my 40s, so relatively late really and even now I'm really keen on getting out on the water as often as I can. The draw for me is the levels of concentration needed, meaning I forget everything that is going on at work. It is a type of therapy. As a person, I like to push myself and so when I was asked to help deliver a yacht across the Atlantic, I did not hesitate. One of the great advantages of being the owner of a business is you can decide things quite quickly and providing the effect is not damaging to the company, you can just take a break. We can all sometimes over analyse things but I knew my team could cope without me, despite the fact there would be no contact for at least two weeks. I also knew that a couple of days of phone calls would be all I needed to get my own project work in order.

Crossing the Atlantic requires planning. Flying to the Canary Islands gave me time to start on my checklist. Rachael, the skipper is a great sailor, ex-military, and a person I trusted but I did not know the rest of the crew. When I agreed to go, I talked to Rachael to check the crew were capable and more importantly to find out if the boat was up to the crossing. Once happy with this, I committed, and started on the more detailed work. It is just about doing your homework and planning the things you should do when embarking on any journey. I gave myself the option to back out once I had met the crew. It would have cost the price of an airline ticket but I was keen to make an informed decision and not pressure myself. I set up a small self-agreement while on the flight over, so I knew when my point of no return was. It was a quick decision originally but I still needed to give myself time and the ability to change my mind once I had all the information.

Rachael gave me the job of victualling (food and other provisions) the boat for the trip and made me first mate. The role formally is second in command but typically it is all about safety and supporting the crew, so that the skipper can focus without distraction. Victualling needed numbers, number of crew x meals per day x days at sea + safety margin. Simple numbers, just the same when planning the early days of your business. How much space do you need, how many phone lines, cell phones, computers, car parking spaces, work benches etc. You can reduce the need by sharing workspace and perhaps introducing shifts but that does depend on what your business does. If you clean domestic windows and share a vehicle, then I'm not sure a night shift will be acceptable to your customers but if you are cleaning office windows, it might be perfect! This is just an example but is the sort of thinking you need to consider when you start.

Drinking water was calculated in litres, per person per day, and then loaded and stowed away in the most efficient way. Then it was preparing for known and unknown variations, lots of treats to keep moral up, lots of games and ideas to relieve boredom. We purchased a fishing rod, downloaded music and films to our devices while we had Wi-Fi onshore. Remember, this is not the safety kit basics because you should know that stuff but when you're running things. You still need to have the money for tea, coffee, toilet paper, paper clips etc. in your office. People are not machine's, so they need to be stimulated. Rachael set up a rota and gave everyone a job title with a set of roles and responsibilities. By managing this early, she empowered people to take responsibility and it made sure everyone was engaged. The crew gave me a list of things they needed to do their roles so that I could add them to my shopping list but also it gave me awareness of what we already had on board and an app was set up on our phones to split the costs. There is so much you can do before your business starts like stock control, accounting, software and IT.

We compiled a pre-departure list. My victualling was checked. I reviewed the navigation plan while the rest of the crew checked each other's jobs, the engine, rigging and toilets etc. We had to back each other up, five people crossing an ocean requires teamwork, something you need to get in place in the early days of your new business.

You will wear lots of hats in the early days, you and your team will need to take holiday for sure, so you need to know each other's roles, and you need to be able to cover and support each other. It was nearly 18 months before I took longer than two consecutive days off work but you cannot expect that from an employee and you should not expect it longer term for yourself.

The next stage meant us taking the boat out to test a new device which had been fitted. We were against the clock, so only had an afternoon. This was one of only two mistakes we made. I am not going into sailing details here but we had an in boom furling system that we struggled to operate correctly. We did work out how to use it but not very well, so perhaps we should have defined specific roles for this slightly more complicated job, even if it meant we would have to wake the crew occasionally, it is something we should have done. This also links to business because it is experience that we learn from a lot of the time. When telling this story in some detail to a friend later on, I remember him saying to me that it was a 'learning opportunity' for future crossings.

Test your own process and product before launching it and if you can, then test it again. Sometimes, you have little choice, but to develop and learn on the job, but you do need to have the principles right. With so much litigation in our culture, you need to be sure what you do is safe. You do not want to start your business with products being returned or to earn a bad reputation for service or quality. A good idea is to test things on friends and family to get honest feedback.

Can you start to see that these are all small steps? We departed, all checked and ready destined for Antigua within two hours of our planned time. The trip would take around 16 days covering 2,700 miles non-stop. Once a boat is a couple of days offshore, the chances of a fast rescue plummet. To give you an idea of the vastness, during our route, we only saw three ships in 16 days.

The rota worked well and every fifth day, one of the five crew was on 'mother watch'. This was a non-sailing day where you would cook, clean, sleep and do your own domestics such as washing clothes and tiding your sleeping area. Rachael and I decided that I would take the first mother watch, why? Firstly, because of moral, I would be off watch only 24 hours after departure, at this time, everyone was still motivated and ready to sail and were not keen to be off watch. The second reason was the main and most important. After the first full night of sailing, the crew were relaxed and had spread their personal kit and equipment all over the boat. This is fine in calm weather, but the term ship shape is about being organised and tidy for when things are not so easy. I had the opportunity to set the standard for this watch and show them what 'good looked like' and what was expected during the trip. I was up with the crew in the morning to make coffee and breakfast. I then cleaned the galley and cleared away personal belongs from the night before. The complete below deck area was cleaned including the heads (toilets). I then planned and agreed lunch with everyone so they knew what time dinner was and what I was cooking before going below and having time to myself to chill out. It was important not to get involved with managing the crew while on mother watch, this was Rachael's role, I needed to stick to my tasks as 'mother', keep everyone supplied with food and drink and chill out and enjoy the ride.

This is exactly what you do as a business grows, you set examples of behaviour. You create a culture and you set out the tasks and requirements for each of the roles you have within your business. It is very easy for people to do what they like doing rather than do what needs to be done as part of their job, so be aware of that.

The crew soon got used to the routine and their responsibilities just like new employees do within a business. Every day on the boat, we had a 15 minute catch up with the crew reporting on their jobs and how they were doing. Sometimes there was not much to report, but it was still done. If anything needed to be completed in the next 24 hours in addition to daily tasks, then that was when we decided when and who would do this. Just like in business, report back to the team and agree any actions.

The only real set back during the trip was a big one. During the first few days, we got caught by a squall at night and because we were not great at furling the main sail our attempt was too late. The weather hit us and destroyed the main sail because we had not got it put away in time. This should have slowed us down but some creativity with our other sails, once it was light, meant we still made good progress. We learnt from it, we reduced the amount of sail we used at night and changed our set up at dusk and dawn each day. On the positive side, nobody was hurt. We did damage a sail but the boat itself was fine. Just like a business you must always be learning and evolving. Safety comes first always; we should have practiced the main sail furling system more.

As the days rolled on, it gave everyone the opportunity to get to know each other and it was interesting how the relationships changed over time. Some of the team were better than others at doing their daily tasks which is completely understandable and it was mine and Rachael's job to keep the important things in check and the moral up, not that moral was really an issue. We always reminded ourselves that the crew were here for fun, so we asked them to do their jobs rather than command it. Not the same at work but a top tip is still to ask for help, even though staff are getting paid and know they have little choice. Rachael had a really nice way of talking to the crew, she was better at it than me, and I thought I was good. Interestingly, we never really managed to get a lot of time together during the crossing because of our roles. As my company grew, the relationship with my fellow directors' changed for the same reasons. Not because of shift patterns but because our roles became more defined and overlapped less.

It was important to remain positive throughout the journey. We had a halfway party and a swim when we were around 1,500 miles from land. Even when the quantity of food was limited, we kept the comments positive, which was relatively easy as the weather improved the closer we got to the Caribbean. Towards the end of our journey, we had spare fresh water, so used it to have a freshwater shower instead of saltwater, which was another small gain and moral boost. All these things broke up the trip. I will not forget the fact that it was made easier by making small steps and small gains. Setting achievable goals is common in business but remembering to review the progress is often forgotten. Sometimes, it is difficult to find the positives, especially if the company is contracting or not winning business but if you continually review and assess there is often a change that can be made to improve things.

One final thing we forgot to add to the plan was the end game. We arrived in Antigua and partied for several days. The rest of the crew stayed on the boat but I checked into a hotel, for which they were all grateful for, as I arranged for everyone's clothes to be washed and they were able to use the Wi-Fi to book flights and plan departures. The owner was planning to join his boat in the Caribbean and in preparation. Rachael really needed all the crew off in good time so she could check, clean and be happy the yacht was in tip top condition for his arrival. What we did not do was make this clear to all the crew early enough. One crewmate stayed on too long and had to be asked to leave, which was an awkward moment. This was our fault. If we had discussed this and told the crew the plan during the trip, we could have easily agreed the number of days in port before the boat had to be vacated. We should have also planned a clean and repair schedule. Doing all of this in advance of arrival would have made things clear and let everyone know where they stood.

During the life cycle of Thinking Space, we have been involved in various partnerships. When they are formed, I am very clear and keen to make sure that everyone knows what the end looks like. People need to know what to do if it goes wrong or if it comes to the end of its natural life. Sometime called an exit strategy, we have known ours from the beginning. Doing this at the start, removes the invested emotion, making the whole process a lot easier.

Can you imagine how much easier Brexit would have been if everyone knew right from the start what the divorce looked like?

It should not be a threat but more of an end of one journey and start of a new one.

I still talk to Rachael and keep in touch with the others from time to time. Crossing the Atlantic was an unforgettable experience for all the right reasons and helped me, not only personally but also in business.

I am planning to do it again very soon.

Chapter Twenty-One
Sandbagging Policeman

What is sandbagging? From a commercial sense, sandbagging is usually done by a salesperson or department. The worst case is when it is done by a sales manager or commercial director. It is the process of hiding orders you receive this month to show next month. You are effectively delaying results.

Let us assume you are a salesperson earning commission on a monthly or quarterly cycle and on the 25th of a month you have done well and have already hit your target. Sandbagging is when you keep the rest of the orders you receive that month in your drawer to help you hit target again the next month. On the face of it, it does not sound like a terrible thing. The salesperson is still working after all, it takes the pressure off a little and, perhaps, even helps with the workload further down the line!

What if I suggest that this activity has a truly massive negative impact on the business? Would you believe me?

The one thing you cannot get back is time and sandbagging sucks days of sales away. When the sales department hit target on 25th, do you think they continued pushing hard on the 26th? They might say they are, but it is not true. They will not push because have already taken the pressure off this month because they have reached target and also taken the pressure off the following month as they have sales to carry forward, effectively a double loss. As entrepreneurs, we are designed to drive forward regardless of the date, so get the orders in, get them processed, then re-set the team and go again. If you must, move the targets and set up a different target system. The more they sell in a month, the bigger their share. It is a difficult balancing act trying to apply positive pressure without putting people under stress but that is the point of the target.

Your job is to become the Sandbagging Police! It is not the sales department's responsibility to worry about other department workloads, so do not let them think they are doing anyone any favours apart from themselves. Believe me, it is better to have too much work than not enough.

The good news is, you now know about 'sandbagging' and you are ultimately equipped to do something about it.

If a sales team are not pushing right up to the last second of the month, then perhaps you do not have the right team in place or the right manager. Sales should be a relentless process. I could write a book just on this subject but for now you must understand that the best salespeople are those who consistently have that drive and are self-starters. Look after them, reward them and train them. You will be surprised how some are not only motivated by money (hey, let us not kid ourselves that is a big factor), but other things such as recognition, personal development and the culture of the business. The days of a dodgy double-glazing or Life Insurance salesperson spending four hours at your kitchen table have nearly gone, thankfully, and that is because businesses do care and have to look after their people and their customers. Most business owners want to build a good reputation and to be known as a good company to deal with and a good employer because it is good for business. The top salespeople have the skills to build relationships, makes sales and leave the customer feeling they were looked after, therefore, recommending you to others. Recommendations can be a valuable part of the pipeline of any business and for my company is one of the key parts. We have satisfied clients who are well-connected and spread good news about our business.

By developing different pipelines of business, you can naturally eliminate the need for sandbagging. We have cultured it out of the business with peer pressure. If a salesperson not only has an order target but targets around quoting, cold calling, visits and new clients, then the salesperson is working right up to deadline day. You just need to have a process in place, not only to verify the performance but systems in place to make it easy to collate the data. What is the point of this information if it takes too much management time and you do not do anything with it when you have it?

Avoid sandbagging, 'count your money when you leave the table and not at the table' as gamblers would say. Keep pushing nonstop and if stress levels go up, then this is something that you need to manage. Take them to the pub or on a day out so they can re-set. Remind them you are all on the same side, sales is not easy but can be a really rewarding field to work in. I remember at one of our family days, one of my sales guys brought his family along and the first thing his wife did was complain to me about his stress levels and working hours. I took it on board and later during the BBQ lunch, we talked again and I told her how valuable he was, how we care and that we work together as a team. I pointed out that the family day organised by the company is one of the ways of thanking her husband, recognising the work he and everyone within the business has done. It was important to me that she felt she could talk to me and I would listen.

I do not believe in keeping people at distance. I do believe in honesty and that keeping people informed of the situation is key. If you find yourself in a situation where you must let someone go or need a discussion about sandbagging, being able to look that person in the eye with integrity is important.

Teamwork and inclusion does have boundaries and limits. Personally, I do not connect with employees on social media. You must be comfortable if you want everyone to know what you get up to outside of work.

Remember sandbagging, I can guarantee at some point you will spot it.

Chapter Twenty-Two
The Fluffy Stuff

I heard this expression in the early days when I attended a sub-contractors show. It was said by one of the delegates who came from one of several old school engineering companies.

Traditional manufacturing companies are notoriously bad when it comes to marketing. Their sales strategy is a rep on the road who is an engineer born and bred with what some would call the 'gift of the gab', usually a guy and usually quite technical. Their marketing effort will be three or four pages of components in a short-printed brochure with a list of machines and the company's quality accreditations. If you are lucky, you also get a photo of the company building and map on the back of where they are.

I wonder if they realised for 30 years, you could hardly tell them apart. I would always smile because you would see the engineers at exhibitions, stood uncomfortably behind a counter displaying a million machined parts, dressed in suits, they would normally only wear to weddings and funerals, with a shirt older than me and their tie undone. To some degree they cannot completely be blamed because as a sub-contractor, selling other people's components, the margins were going to be relatively tight, so this would have had an effect on the sales and marketing spend. There are ways to be effective on a budget but sometimes the culture of a business is difficult to change.

I am from that world originally but saw it as a sector with lots of opportunity, simply because the approach to sales and marketing was behind the times and very disjointed. The positive thing about this sector was when working with engineers you knew where you stood. They usually knew what they wanted and if they did not, they would tell you. The amount of time wasted was minimalised because they understood the value of time, including the time put in by a salesperson, which is not considered in a lot of industries.

So, this is how you explain 'fluffy stuff'. The last thing a traditional engineer wants to manage is something un-tangible. A marketing plan or strategy was often regarded as 'fluffy Stuff'.

So why is the 'Fluffy stuff' important. Let us talk in more detail about the importance of acknowledging this and including it in your plans. Marketing is a prime example and when used well, it is not 'fluffy' at all. Marketing is not just about setting up a website and attending an exhibition. For me, it is much more than that. The tangible work is easy. You can see it, read it and feel it but the real skill in marketing when it is a driving force in the company's DNA. When you break it down, you will find it common sense and logical. Unless you are well-funded in the early days. There is little chance of you appointing a marketing manager but the good news is, the marketing industry seems to have a large pool of part time professionals and small independent businesses. A lot of small companies need part time support, finding good people able to work on a retainer or part time is a good option. Being a business with its own products and a wide range of services, marketing was important to us and this led us to recruiting a full-time employee quite early in our growth.

Marketing is driven by the company's objectives to get its products and services to the right people. That all comes from the business plan for growth. Information comes from the sales history or research you have. It comes from the skills, the products and services you provide and, goes around in a continuous circle. Marketing needs to pull that all together. It helps you focus on the right customers you want to talk to or the sectors you want to work in. Remember, marketing is largely about helping you sell more product.

So, how did we embrace it? We generated a lot of data and information, not only about our customers but our business internally. We could more accurately record and process information about our own manufacturing, such as which product could be produced the most efficiently and which required the most investment in time. We worked out what sectors of industry had the fastest quote to order time and which ones made the most money. This knowledge is gold but is worthless unless you act upon its information.

One of my business partners, Paul Atkins, is not the marketing fluffy type at all. Paul was converted to the benefits of quality marketing because of what our commercial teams did with this raw data. The directors could accurately direct the sales and marketing team, where to focus their efforts at specific times, often towards the more profitable sectors. If we won some very labour-intensive work, we would direct the marketing department to focus on the basic, simpler work that we still had capacity for. Sounds simple and it is. The skill is how the marketing effort is directed. There must be a plan or a campaign, the advertising, branding, sales, products and service levels, all need to tie together. You might get some joy from a web site or an occasional exhibition but if you have a marketing plan, the returns will be greater for sure.

I have made broad brush statements that certain types of manufacturing engineering companies do not invest in marketing. I personally think this is often because it is not easy to measure and as a mechanical guy myself, I do see their point. However, if you measure the commercial performance of a business, the 'fluffy stuff' can enhance your reputation on its own. A great example I can give you here is in the automotive sector. The most unreliable cars in the UK according to independent surveys at the moment include all the brands linked with quality. Mercedes, BMW, Jaguar and Land Rover. So why do people perceive them as quality brands? Great marketing.

Let us look at another example. Networking. Networking is part of marketing and sales. It assists in the development of the business and should therefore be included in your business plan. When the firm was growing, I could never get across to Paul the importance of networking. After over 18 years of working together, he is still not a fan but I now know he values it. He just delegates it to me and the commercial director.

The reason why it has to be part of a plan is because some areas are more fun and easier to do than others and there is a risk you will spend your time doing the easier tasks rather than those that pose more of a challenge. It is also important not to spend too much time on something that will not help the business today. Remember Jam tomorrow? You must invest a little in everything but not too much into something that will not affect you today.

Networking is another good example of this.

To sell a product or service efficiently, you try to reach your target customer, namely the ones who have a need for it. For example, if you are trying to sell a car share scheme, you could focus on people in built up areas where they have limited space to park their own car. If you were selling or hiring out bouncy castles on the other hand, you would not focus on this group but on those that have the space.

In the early days I would attend a lot of networking events especially in the evenings when it made me feel like I was still working but not impacting my core time. Local accountants, banks, law firms would use them to bring companies together. I joined the IOD (Institute of Directors) to meet likeminded people. Their networking events consisted of a bacon roll and a cup of coffee at a hotel. There was usually a guest speaker who presented for 20 minutes and then there was the opportunity to chat to other delegates. There were other more formal events but it was all about meeting people. After a time, I found I was meeting the same people at each event and it became less effective for me.

I remember on one occasion, I had a real disagreement with a small business owner. I cannot remember what he did but in his opinion the way to grow his business was through networking events. Contacts can be made and you can win work but because of the random nature of some networking events, the route to the customer is too speculative and too inefficient. You would need a super product with universal demand for networking to be the answer on its own and he did not have this. He did not have the ability to find, contact, call and talk to customers over the phone. It is not an easy thing to do, which I understand but, remember, if you do not have the skill to do something, acknowledge it and buy it in. If you cannot call a potential client and try to build a relationship with a stranger, then you need someone who can because all customers start out as strangers.

Your time is so important, so when attending any event, you need to maximise the opportunity.

Networking can have a plan of its own and each event needs a plan. You need to know why you are attending, what is the objective, who do you want to talk to and what do you want to talk about. In the early days you could have several reasons for attending events. It may be that the guest speaker is influential in the industry you want to get close to, so you are hoping to learn something and make some good contacts. You might be looking for a person to solve a problem or perhaps help you supply something or may use them for recruitment.

Make sure that your time is spent in a managed way doing different things that can impact your business positively over time. For example, if you are attending a networking event because it is good to have your brand associated with the organiser, think about how long it will take for you to reap that benefit? If you cannot cover the bills until that benefit pays, then forget it, do it later when you can invest the resources, in this case, your time.

There are a few things you can do to help make your networking successful. Do your homework, find out who is going to be at the event, ask the organiser if they have a list of delegates, review it, take notes and take these with you. People like talking about themselves and if you know what they do and show interest, they will remember you. There is no excuse for a lack of research because the internet is full of information.

List who you want to talk to while you are there and also what you are going to talk about. Do you have an ice breaker or linking introduction from someone else? Networking is informal by nature, but you will do better if you are well-presented, so make sure you are clean, tidy, and smell nice. Set yourself a challenge of trying to speak to all the contacts on your list, once you have made contact, then you can follow this up with a call after the event. Do not pounce or be pushy and do not force your sales literature upon them or go into selling mode.

Try to work the room (get around all of it), one way to do this is play the host. I have done this a lot of times and it works really well. Stand by the coffee machine and poor drinks, it is instantly a way of saying hello. If you cannot find someone on your list, then ask the organisers for a description or introduction. Have a short 'elevator pitch' ready to use. This is a short description of what your company does explained in such a way that any listener can understand it in a short period of time. Look online for some examples of this.

Carry a near empty cup around. It is a great excuse to leave a group or conversation if it is not interesting to you because you can make an excuse and go and get a top up. When you go for a top up, wait until someone you do not know is at the coffee area so you can play host for them. Even better if there is a queue because you have a captive audience of people waiting. Ask open questions and use open body language.

You are more approachable if you are stood alone. If you are engaged in intense conversation, people will tend not to approach. If you attend the event with a colleague, then split up to maximise your time to ensure you engage with all those on your list.

If the event is reasonably well-organised, then there is often a seating plan. If you have not managed to catch someone during the day or do not know who they are, then find out where they are sitting. Check who they are talking to, perhaps you know them and can ask them to introduce you. Charm the organiser, often they are only too pleased to help and can introduce you or sit you on the right table.

Always take a nice notebook and make notes actively in front of people. If nothing else, it will keep you engaged especially if the speaker is boring or if the subject is just dull. I have spent many networking events listening to the poorest speakers about the most uninteresting subjects but just have a think about what the other delegates will feel about you if you are engaged and taking notes. You will come over as professional and it suggests to people you are also busy. It also gives people an opportunity to open a conversation with you if you are seen taking notes and in return you can ask people about specific subjects that have been discussed. It's a win-win. Just remember one thing, if all you did was write down your weekly shopping list, just make sure people cannot see it.

If the event goes on into the evening and you find yourself at the bar with a glass of wine, remember you are still working. You do not want people to remember you for the wrong reasons. Even in the bar, make an assessment as to whether you should be drinking wine, beer or a soda!

My final tip is to make sure you have plenty of business cards with you and if someone hands you theirs, then do not be afraid to write a note on it to remind you who they were or what you discussed.

20 years of networking has really paid off for me, but it is one part of a complete strategy. My commercial director is very good at networking customers. He knows a lot of people and as part of our marketing strategy and product positioning, clients recognise us both and come back. It is great when you are introduced to someone because you were recommended. It is also great if you forward or introduce a client to one of your suppliers or customers. It is all part of networking. Paul can pass on project information in return for details about business we are not aware of. Not all our sales guys are naturals when it comes to networking, so remember the 'right person, right box' chapter here.

I use networking differently nowadays, as the MD, Chairman, CEO I can now build up contacts on a different level. When my team need advice and expertise, I usually know someone who can help. I try to attend one a month. My work includes amongst other things, supporting local education establishments, so when needed, I can call on a large network of contacts and they can call on me.

When traveling, I try to never eat alone. There is always an engineer or contact that would happily come to dinner. If the conversation dries up, have some ideas of things you can talk about. I use football a lot – when travelling internationally, I am often asked who I support. My mission is to remember what their team is and be prepared the next time we meet. As I have said before people like to talk about themselves, so ask open questions and stay interested with eye contact and body language.

Before you know it, you are a networking pro.

Chapter Twenty-Three
You are not Pizza

I read this expression on a web site and it made me smile. It works on the theory that everyone loves pizza. You are not pizza, so not everyone loves you! It is such a great analogy.

But why do some people not like me? I am perfect, right? Sadly, not!

During the course of running your business, you will upset some and there will be others you do not get on with or who do not get on with you. There are a number of techniques that can be used to minimise any pain and conflict but sometimes you will find some individuals just do not warm to you and they are not likely to tell you they do not like you. They will tend to disengage and not respond rather than be confrontational. It does not mean the person hates you. It just means they would rather communicate with somebody else. If you can work out why the person is not warming to you, there is a chance you can save the situation from a business perspective. I am not talking about some sort of personality switch or a change in your core behaviour, but you can work things out.

The wonderful thing about being the boss is that you can choose who you work with and for, and we have chosen on a couple of occasions not to work with someone. Sometimes, you have little choice because winning work might be more important. Turning someone down can be done directly or you can simply price yourself out of the market and/or offer a long lead time. By taking this approach, the refusal is commercial and not personal.

When faced with a relationship or communication challenge, try to simply understand it and accept it. There will be moments you will not win business because of it. This might not be because the client dislikes you but perhaps they prefer to deal with a competitor more. If you can find out why they prefer the competitor, then this is something you can work on, so take a positive from it.

Review your standards, check your processes and double check your approach. A good salesperson changes their approach and style according to each person they interact with and in line with their needs and the environment. I really enjoy watching a good salesperson at work. They ask open questions, they learn, they probe and then they use what they have found out to meet the customer's requirements because they have developed a relationship and understanding. Understanding the customer's needs is key to a sales relationship. What is the point of talking about your amazing range of colours when the most important thing to the client is the fire rating or the warrantee period? Each client has a different set of needs and a good salesperson selects the correct information to meet each need. This is not the 'gift of the gab' as I was told I had for many years. It is the experience gained from watching others and the professional training received. I have even used this training in social situations when meeting someone for the first time, especially at group events where you are introduced to several new people together.

Your business will have products or services available and the skill is matching the needs of your customers to these products/services. By doing this, you will be able to help solve their problems and start to build trust and a relationship. If it works, you are 'pizza'.

A salesperson with a good relationship can give both good and bad news to a client without too much trouble but one technique that can be used in a situation where perhaps the relationship is formal or new, is what I call the third-party blame. This method should not be used a lot as it does go somewhat against the teamwork spirit within the business but a good time to use it is around payment terms. The third-party blame removes you as the barrier. For example, if we get a call stating that payment terms are 90 days from delivery and we do not want to accept that, the rep can make a call and blame a third party, which would usually be me. "I'm sorry, Mr Customer, but the MD says you can only have 30 days." If the customer is not happy with this, it allows the rep to continue with, "let me talk to him for you and see what I can arrange." The rep then talks to me and we agree a better term but one we are still happy with. The rep has created a level of trust and can usually back everything up because it is true and not a fabrication. Another suggestion is to provide evidence and the good thing about the internet is that it often contradicts itself and in this situation, it can help. Even if the client has a good credit score on one web site, it will be average or missing a score from another, so if the client wants an explanation why they cannot have full credit, show them the site that their score is poor on. Never lie, if you want to build a relationship, you need trust.

I will never forget a big presentation I did in Saudi Arabia in front of the heads of the Aviation authority. I was one of three companies asked to attend a meeting about our solution. The other presenters were not competitors but potential partners within the group we would have to work with. One was a provider of special HD screens and another was a systems integration firm. We were invited by a prime contractor to help him win the overall project from a major government department. I had done my homework on who I was presenting to and worked out this was high level so they would not want technical detail (although I would have it just in case), but would expect an overview demonstrating value and quality. My presentation needed to be engaging rather than lots of spreadsheets, showing what the solution would look like and convincing them we were a partner they would want to work with. My presentation was planned to be last. This could be good or bad. If the others took too long, then I might have a shorter time and if they are not engaging, the clients could already be on their phones planning the rest of their meetings. On the plus, it gave me time to assess things, make sure the IT was working and make any tweaks on my presentation, based on questions, feedback and my own thoughts on how it was going.

The systems company went first, big corporate power point presentation. It was formal but focused on their specific project. It was good and I was frantically thinking how I was going to match it for quality and detail. I did not need to worry because the second guy stood up and killed us all with his presentation. I will never forget his last five slides (yes, five). They were all about packaging. Now if this client had been remotely interested in green issues or we were in a region where the transport infrastructure was poor, I could understand it but he just seemed to be delivering a presentation used many times over, which had obviously not been tailored for this meeting.

He finished and I looked at the customers (for the first time in 15 minutes), they had nearly lost the will to live! (I knew I had). I needed a change of tact to bring them back. I investigated my 'tool bag', stood up, grabbed some physical material samples and was on a mission to firstly make sure we both liked 'pizza'. I got their attention by putting on a short video about Thinking Space, nothing corporate or formal but one about how and where we started and about the amount of tea we drink on a daily basis! I turned the sound down and using open body language, narrated it to give it more oomph but did this not from the lectern but from the edge of the four-person desk they were sat at. I then showed them big images of their project and how it was going to look when completed. I talked about us working together. I mentioned the number of times I had been to the Kingdom and how I knew they liked tea as much as me! They warmed to me, I was 'pizza' and we won the business. The trick is to use the correct tools in your bag for each occasion.

If you are not Pizza, what else can you do, and why can you not just change your toppings to be loved by everyone? Unless you are a split personality, you are going to struggle. For me, relationships are a journey and people can certainly warm to you over time. Time is a factor because if you are seen at events one after the other, it bounds reassurance that you will still be around long after the project. One option if you don't have a good relationship is to pass the sales contact over to a colleague as they may have more success. It is something we have done a couple of times over the years. What is interesting is that chances are your fellow salespeople are also like you because we recruit people we like, which is a challenge. When there is more of a HR structure in place in the company, this can get eliminated but perhaps it is also why a lot of companies have middle-aged, white fat men at the top because that is who employed them! When people realise it is not good for business perhaps diversity will finally be embraced more. Personally, I feel a diverse workforce is great for business, we have a lot of nationalities within the company and although we only have a handful of women, most of them are in the management team. Perhaps the way for the business to be pizza is to have a diverse team.

When you realise you are not a client's first choice, remember it is only work but don't give up. I have some great customers now, who openly say they were not keen when we started talking because they considered me a little brash and pushy. In my defence, it is not easy to be charismatic when you need work to pay your mortgage. Have integrity and honesty if you can in business as it will help with relationships. Never get drunk in front of a customer regardless of the situation. Never speak out of turn about suppliers, competitors or projects even if it has upset you.

Employing a person you do not warm to is really difficult but as long as you are confident they will fit into the team, then do it. As a new small business, you cannot spend a lot of time trialling candidates but never rule out a person just because their style is different to yours.

My business partners and I are constantly matching customers to our staff. We always try to make sure the people match to aid communication. I am not talking about a female client needs a female contact, I am talking more about the psychology of sales here. We do have customers who only want to deal with the Boss but that is changing. I have never found a man asking to talk to another man but apparently it happens in other industries but I have seen advantages of local knowledge and language skills. For example, Germans do like to deal with Germans. It does not rule you out if you are French but it is worth understanding. We have clients that want to discuss things over a coffee informally and then some that want to test your technical knowledge. Our job is to pair these people up to the correct contacts within our company.

Sales and communication can be taught. They are great skills to have, so keep training yourself and your teams with the latest techniques. Keep putting tools into their 'tool bag' but above everything else, never forget that you might not appeal to everyone…you are not pizza.

Chapter Twenty-Four
Don't Forget FIFA

I'm a massive football fan. I played until I was too old to carry on but passed this passion on to my children. Nothing highlights business actions in a 'how not to' way than some of the actions of the governing body, FIFA. This chapter is not about public relations or about management, it is all about one thing that is more common than you might think.

I am talking about corruption and the first thing you need to be aware of is that it can be found in every country and in all walks of business life, even if it is only on a very low level. I was quite naïve to this when I first came into business. You need to be aware that it goes on but not get involved in it. Have integrity and if you must, just play dumb. Pretend you do not understand and ensure that all agreements made can be backed up with supporting documentation.

The last chapter talked about the 'pizza' idea where sometimes you just won't get on with a person for whatever reason. This is a little different in that. Sometimes the deal is already done behind closed doors and it makes no difference what you say or what you do. Over the years of running my companies, I have seen it in so many different forms, from subtle moments in a process negotiation, right through to being asked for cash and goods on the back of orders being placed.

I choose FIFA as an example because they are in the public eye for all the wrong reasons around corruption. Can you imagine what goes on behind closed doors if corporations are not in the public eye? Sometimes it is not easy to spot corruption but it is fascinating to me now that I have some experience of it. Spotting it can be an art. Other times, it is so much in your face that you still miss it.

I have lost business and not even been invited to tender massive UK projects because of corruption. One of the companies was even partly government owned. To lose a contract because of a back handed deal is completely demoralising, particularly when you have invested time and money in the tender process. I have been knowingly caught out by it three times and I would rather have been told from the start that we were not going to win, so that I could have invested my time in other work. All three times it was either for a government authority or a global well known 'blue chip' company. .

My tip is never 'burn your bridges'. Speaking out would end any work between my company and the client and with no idea who is connected to it, you could upset a lot of people. Some successful people abuse their power and some are just greedy. Learn from it and move on.

I was a local supplier for a major government funded UK company. We were beating the existing supplier on every project, partly because we were physically well-positioned and also because the original supplier appeared to have wound down operations. We were winning larger and larger projects but were still waiting for a capital contract to come our way. A major refit was looming so we worked hard to be fully engaged before the tender process began. One mistake we made was the lengths we went to before the project was awarded. I attended various sites whenever asked, often at short notice and completed a lot of small projects for next to no charge in an effort to build the relationship. To give you an idea of the scale, the project was worth the equivalent of a year's work for us! We thought the competitor had gone bust because we were not aware of any projects or clients they were working with for the year running up to the project. One afternoon, I get a call from purchasing wanting to arrange a meeting. I thought this is it. Here is the opportunity to get some designs across and really show them what we can do. We sat down and talked about some minor work and I was asked to provide a free design for another tiny room. I was happy to do this but asked what was happening about the main suite. The response was that the decision had been made a while ago and an order had been placed with another supplier, he added, "If you can complete a design for this, then let us see how you do." The purchasing guy could not look me in the eye and ended the meeting promptly, so I could not cross-examine him. He was clearly embarrassed. The feeling I got was this small design project was our 'compensation'. I could do nothing except learn from it. The project had not even gone to full tender, so we were not able to put in a bid. Without a shadow of a doubt, someone very senior was being looked after. I found out a year later that the consoles supplied were double our listed prices and I can say that three years later, I still know of no other clients the contractor has worked for before or since.

I kept the relationship going and put it down to experience. I must admit I did talk to a legal friend but we agreed that it would not be beneficial to anyone for us to formally complain. On the plus side it has made me more confident to ask quite difficult questions during the early stages of a project. I have been known to ask if it is really a live project or just an exercise. When questioned on why I ask, I simply say we are a small business with limited resources and we only want to propose projects we actually have a chance of winning!

What I'm not talking about and certainly not concerned about are low level sweeteners. For me, this is part of building a relationship and making a deal. I have no problem with some corporate entertaining or free pens, note pads and the odd social lunch. That for me is not what we are talking about here. Getting to know a customer is great and developing trust is part of business so always be happy to buy dinner.

This chapter is about where to expect corruption and how to navigate it. Sometimes, you might be asked to be complicit! That will test your moral compass for sure!

A tell tail sign of where to expect corruption is when you are dealing with a person who does not take responsibility for the money. For example, when you are dealing with a special project that is of unusually high value. If middle or junior managers are suddenly involved with the decision making on a major investment, the opportunity for a sweetener appears. You could be called into a meeting and a manager in the team could ask if he can help you in any way. They might tell you that they are here to help and support the smooth running of the project, so feel free to approach them! They can help iron out any snags later, perhaps, but what they are really saying is look after me today and I will look after you tomorrow. If you are in a meeting alone, when there are usually a number of people involved, you have a good warning right there.

Other times it is less subtle. I remember a project manager midway through a job sending me a link to a new iPhone and asking me what I thought of the latest design as he was looking to get one! He even put his home address on the bottom of the email.

My top tip is to put everything on email. Do not threaten to go public or anything like that but keep bringing the conversation back to the job in hand.

You can always say there is not enough money in the project for extras but sometimes that can backfire! I was once about to be given an order for £100k and the person raising the order asked me to send a quote for £105k, which they would raise an order for. They explained they expected the job quoted would overrun and so this would cover any incidentals. Sounds credible enough but later, I was sent a link to a 50" TV and a delivery address. I sent back a formal order acceptance to their business email (but only to them), I then had an email back advising it was no longer required!

Another way to deal with this is to pass it up the line. As the managing director, principal or CEO (whatever title you like), you are regarded as the final decision maker but you can always mention the 'Company Secretary'. It is an old title and many years ago they were required to sign off your accounts and a legal requirement to be a named person within the business. That is no longer the case but I do sometimes use the 'I need to talk to my company secretary' line if required. Because you are going to share and formalise the request, the client suddenly has a change of heart.

Just remember that a bribe or 'backhander' as it used to be called can be quite subtle. The trick is to be aware it goes on and that in some countries it could be part of everyday life and not unusual. Do not let it upset you. If you are offered something 'special' or are invited to be part of a non-standard offer, be aware and cautious. If you want to get out of the situation, ask them to provide details and clarification of what they are asking for in an email, quite often they will then back down. Try not to overreact, be angry or surprised, just be aware it goes on and take it in your stride.

I was amazed that people were surprised about corruption allegations in 'FIFA'. Think about the sums of money involved and the type of people at the head of the business. Does it not stand out as obvious with the way the organisation is set up and the need to win votes to host a world cup from heads of other national football associations? We have world cups coming up in Russia and Qatar that were voted for ahead of some of the biggest footballing countries who wanted to host.

We now have scandals and investigations at massive blue-chip firms such as Siemens and Rolls Royce. I truly hope it decreases, otherwise only the big companies will prosper. Some business markets are more prone to bribes than others. I remember a building friend having a hot tub delivered to his house by a plumbing company, they had 'over stocked' and it was spare!

What is positive is that some countries are really trying to eradicate it. Some of the fines issued are eye watering and the reputations of companies can be ruined. On the negative side, when we have dealt with countries with a history such as Italy, the amount of paperwork and form filling is so big it can then rule you out of a project altogether. I have lost two projects in Portugal that by law have to be open to European companies but we had no chance because the documents were required to have local authorisation stamps.

Always try to set the right tone in your business and develop a culture from the top. Try to lead by example. Make people aware and do not be a company that offers bribes. It is slippery slope.

Chapter Twenty-Five
Exit This Way

If only we knew what the end looked like! If we know when we were going to die, for example, then we could plan our lives. Our money would last and we could say goodbye and generally get things in order. You could live fully and productively until the end.

Whenever you start a company, always have a think about what the end looks like. We have talked about business plans what I am talking about now is the last five years. Yes, to exit a business could take that long but it is not just about the end game, this process has to be thought about at the start and when going into anything like a business partnership, you should agree how you can get out of it! When you start a company (unlike a marriage), you do not expect to die holding the hand of it do you?

From bitter experience I can tell you how easy it is to 'cock this up' and that is even if you think you had a plan!

You might just want to hand your company down to family or to your management team or even just close it and walk away but whatever you decide, you need to prepare and prepare those that are involved. There are lots of ways to both prepare your business for sale and maximise its value.

Over the years we have been involved with acquisitions from time to time. My business is relatively risk adverse. We know what we are good at so we always look for something that has a bit of a track record and perhaps can be improved with the introduction of skills of our own. It makes us the same as most other SME's (small to medium Enterprises) that want to have a go at buying another business. A lot of SME's are owner managed where the founder wants to exit (usually retire). It is not an ideal place to be in when you come to sell because of the risk involved to the buyer. A risk to a buyer reduces the value.

Imagine you have run a great business for years. It is profitable and has a good customer base. After 25 years you decide you want to sell up, it is time to relax and work your way through that bucket list. The firm must be valuable because it makes money, right? As a buyer I would want to know who within the company has the skills to cover what you do when you are sat in the club house. How many of your customers are going to look elsewhere once you go because you have been looking after them for so long and are their only point of contact? How much company information is in your head and not written down, documented or recorded? In addition, there is the effect on the remaining staff, will they leave when you do? It all adds up to risk for the person buying and that will mean either a lower price or no sale.

Consider this, if you get halfway through the life of the company and you tell everyone that in ten years you are going to retire, what affect does that have? I can tell you from our own experience. It is positive (albeit a little weird), particularly if your exit gives more than just a date, but a plan of who is going to do what. If your plan details how much money you want to take with you that you want to go down to three days a week and then one, would that company not be worth so much more? This is not about the management training or the mechanics of work, it is about leaving. If you can agree the notice period and how you are going to calculate the money from the start, then things will be so much smoother.

This is not just about retirement but about all contracts or relationships that need to end at some time. If you have a deal with a contractor or a consultant and things change and you do not want to continue, how much easier would it be if there was a clear exit.

I have heard stories about companies, who when they set up their firms, already knew the type of buyer they would appeal to and worked throughout their growth to get close and to appeal to the target buyer. I have never managed to do this but it is a good idea even if the buyer is a daughter or nephew!

I have two fellow directors with shares within my business and I expected that two of us would retire together handing over the company to the third partner who is ten years younger. It did not quite work out like that because Paul decided he wanted to stop work earlier. We did not have a plan at the time but we are friends and we knew it would be a process we needed to work through and, fortunately, he gave us a really long notice period so we could plan. This was not a completely selfless thing for him to do. He also wanted to maximise his value, so the more time we had, the more chance we had of reaching his value expectations.

What I had done a few years previously, was to tie the three of us to a share contract. I remember at the time Paul questioned my desire to do this because he felt it suggested a lack of trust. I trusted him completely but decided to formalise things before they became important. I am glad I did it as it crystallised the negotiation process later and gave us a basic starting point. In theory it limited our options a little on who we could sell shares to and what the options were. I would not say the process was easy but having some foundations and with all parties wanting a solution, it was always going to work out. There can be a lot of emotion involved. Remember, this is the final pay-out to the owner or partner so it is important. They may have been working their whole life for this.

I have never stopped trusting or respecting Paul and the good work he has done. The business is better with him in it and I am a better person with him as a friend and colleague, so the last thing I want is to end our working relationship in any other way than as friends. What has worked is the fact that we have plenty of time to talk and plan before his departure. The other good decision we made was to use our accountancy firm to mediate for us, as this kept things moving and we both trusted our accountant. I have a single ambition that Paul comes out of the business happy, wealthy, positive and feeling that I looked after him as much as he looked after me.

I will talk about how you set your 'moral compass' at the end of this book but for me it is not all about the money. I must be comfortable with myself at the end of my career and think I strived to be a good employer and business partner. You should too. I am definitely not perfect and, hey, if you do not give a shit, you might earn more money but it helps me sleep at night and will help you! This book is not just about making money, it is about helping you navigate the challenges and why we are doing this. A big factor is that you must enjoy the journey.

Chapter Twenty-Six
Around the World

I often get asked, "Just how did you get the business exporting so well and how did you get things moving?" This chapter is all about how 30% of what we do is now exported, how we ended up importing two major products and why we decided to do that in the first place!

Some parts of international business appear very cool, lots of long-haul flights to exotic locations, all your friends on social media commenting on the great life you have and always asking where you are going next. The reality in the early days is completely different. Business travel was red eye night flights, always economy class and seeing nothing other than industrial estates and offices during the trip. Some trips I would not leave the airport because the work was based there. Nowadays when I travel, I always try to give myself an extra 24 hours wherever I am just to either re-charge the batteries or check out a city before returning home. At the start I could not afford to do that.

I spent a lot of time emailing and calling anyone linked to the industry and I built up great contacts with various business support authorities, both locally and internationally, as well as with end users and integrators. I was mad hungry for growth. One evening when I was surfing the internet, I came across a government web site that supported UK business for export. Back then it was the United Kingdom Trade for Industry (UKTI). I filled in some forms, made a few calls, then finally a meeting was arranged.

A demure lady, called Rosalind Marsh from UKTI, came to the barn, our first workshop, to tell us all about the government support program for business regarding export. At the time I would not have thought we would get on so well but Rosalind helped me and the business for the next 15 years until she retired. At first, Rosalind just asked what our plan was, which was easy, the plan was world domination! She said, "Well, how are you going to achieve that?"

She told me I needed a plan, We had a plan and that included being able to export the product and create a solution that could be built on site by local people with minimal or no tools and skills. What I did not have was a bigger strategy around marketing, agents and distributors (I do now, for sure). Rosalind gave me a rundown of various grants and support packages. One option was a 'Trade Mission' organised by various sectors. Because we cover lots of sectors including Air Traffic and Security, we could happily sit within different grants. Over the years, what Rosalind did was constantly look for opportunities, training and grants that would help us. She would even fill in some of the forms to make sure we ticked the correct boxes. There are lots of grants available from various government bodies. Some are hard to get because there is so much bureaucracy and form filling involved sometimes not making it worth the hassle but Rosalind helped remove that. I recommend you find a Rosalind of your own.

We attended some training organised via the UKTI which was OK. Training provided by government bodies can be hit and miss and just as I was deciding not to attend anymore "free" seminars the UKTI advertised one regarding agents and distributors. It was probably the best single days training I have ever had. I liked the idea of a trade mission that Roz had suggested and managed to get one that coincided with an exhibition, so rather than just going to check out a country, we could exhibit at the same time maximising the value of the trip. The country we selected was Dubai.

So why Dubai? Simple, the price of a cup of coffee (market research)! When we pick a country to work in, the first test is the price of the coffee! This is about the amount people are willing to pay. If people are used to paying a lot for a coffee, then they are used to paying the proper money for things including consoles. In real terms, we also checked to see if there was any local competition and checked to ensure the exhibition itself was well supported and established. Was there a market for what we do? Rosalind got us a grant that matched our investment, so off we went to Dubai on our first ever international business trip.

We took the red-eye flight because it was cheap and reduced hotel costs. We stayed in an out-of-town hotel and quickly learnt that the all you can eat breakfast buffet was your main meal of the day. That first trip was so interesting, standing on a booth with a dozen posters around me talking to people. This was my hunting ground. I took my new business partner and it gave me the opportunity to impress him. The first trip to Dubai taught me so much about international work. I am still learning today. I was a little worried that I was being cheeky using the government grant to help me partly fund the exhibition, but I should not have worried. It was quite clear that upon meeting other delegates on the trade mission that some of the companies were just on a government assisted holiday. How some of these businesses qualified for a grant amazed me.

The fact the UK government was not getting great value upset me at the time, but not as much as meeting people at the British embassy! We were required to attend a function where the trade delegation met local business experts. Sounded like a great idea and how very nice to attend an event at the local embassy,. On arrival I got a special badge because I was considered a local expert because I was at the exhibition. After talking to the genuine 'local businesses', it was clear that the same ones were rolled out at each event. They just looked like civil servants attending for a free lunch. The next day we attended a conference where the Embassy business development staff gave us their expertise and training on 'working in the UAE'. It was OK but not particularly inspiring and three years later after many trips to the UAE, I attended the same event only to find them delivering exactly the same presentation. Apparently, embassy staff are rotated every three years, how can they gain real local knowledge and expertise? How can they develop good business contacts? Experience has shown that some government departments and embassy's work better than others. Ask some difficult questions and you will quickly work out who is who.

The trip was a success and we collected over 60 contacts and produced 12 quotes for projects from the show. It took hours of work following up and building relationships with these contacts. We were not ready for that the first year but we certainly were the next year. It is an old saying but when you start out, go for the low hanging fruit, go after the work you know you can win and for us that was really in the UK. Attracting international business requires several trips and must be part of a planned investment. It took many years and a lot more time and money than expected, but we got there in the end.

While at the show we had lots of people asking to be our agents. Never go into this lightly. I remember one man saying he represented lots of companies, his business card stated he could sell you anything from a fax machine to a firearms! I kept the card for years because it actually had various photos on the back including a printer and an AK47!

Top tip here, if you are going to select someone to represent you, make sure they are picking you because of your product. If they have complementary services that tie into what you do, then great but a small company with lots of arms means some things are not being worked on.

Rosalind introduced me to embassies in every country I visited. Some were good and some not so but to have people know you could only be positive. I got to know people in many different countries and when traveling alone, I found it a comfort to meet a friendly face for a coffee or dinner. Do not underestimate the power of hosting a meeting at the embassy. I remember one embassy allowing me to use a meeting room for a day and the visitors clearly enjoyed it, particularly that they needed a formal invite to get past security. The room was fantastic with pictures of the queen everywhere to top it off. It gave me, as a new business, some status and credibility.

During the first exhibition in Dubai, I was given a memory stick by one customer detailing drawings of a project. My only problem was that I did not have a laptop! At that time we really couldn't afford one and relied on our phones for emails. Another tip here is, make friends with your fellow exhibitors, our neighbour kindly downloaded the data, then emailed it to me so that I could get it printed out at the hotel. The customer asked me to attend a meeting at the airport the following day. I will never forget being up half the night trying to remember if he said gate two terminal three or gate three terminal two! I got up early the next day and grabbed a cab telling the driver my problem! He smiled and said, "It's not a problem, sir, the airport only has two terminals, so let us go to T2 gate three." He got a good tip. Of course, another tip here is to make clear notes when talking to a client!

Our events are now very well-organised. Once you get a feel for the different nationalities, you do start to develop more relationships and learn how each one works. It sounds like I am creating stereotypes, but different cultures and nationalities do have traits you need to learn.

Because we have mentioned it already, let us talk about the Middle-East. No question there is wealth and much of it, I would suggest many countries are, more liberal than you would expect. Just respect the different cultures and you will be fine. You could almost mistake some of the cities as western with their big shopping malls, including many chain stores we all know with a Starbucks and KFC on every corner. Some basic facts to start, there is a massive, truly massive gap between people with money and people without. That is generally not good. In business, it means lots of middle managers because wages at the bottom are low, so there are a lot of people trying to be involved, earning little money and having little responsibility. The UAE is not a democracy which has a bearing on how they do business. Only 10% of the population are nationals which means that 90% of the time you are dealing with lots of different people/cultures from other countries. As a rule, building trust takes time and so decisions are slow. With so many management layers there is a possible element of corruption, which we have already covered, so be aware of this.

Trust must be built for one main reason with so many people involved, nobody takes responsibility through fear of being wrong (or actually having any authority). It means you can have a green light to make something but still find out later it is not what they expected.

A customer that I had met whilst at an exhibition came to visit us the following year at that time we were located in a barn. The car they drove down in was worth more than my business at the time. Clearly, we were not ready for them then and the look on their faces meant we were not going to win the work despite my efforts to provide clean cups and expensive coffee. I did try hard to impress them and to some degree it changed my approach to international work. Interestingly, 20 years later we did get the project when it came up for renewal. I did not recognise any of the guys from the first visit but I would say that is a good testament to how we have developed as a company over that period.

In the UAE, each level of manager wants to add value so be prepared to be asked for a discount and some degree of change from each person involved. One challenge is there are some roles filled by people that really do not have a lot to do. They are paid but the training and development structures are not in place. Some lower managers do not want the responsibility and are not that skilled. I truly love the UAE to travel and work in. It is changing so quickly, every time I go, I see the investment working and the skills and companies improving.

When we win projects, it is common for customers to inspect the work at our factory in England. When you take this on, it is not just the cost of the hotels and the transfers that you need to consider but also the admin time to get visas and the fact they might not all travel together. Those more senior may stay longer (usually in London). It is also common for those coming from the Middle-East to want to visit friends as many will have been educated in the UK. It is really positive that our universities are highly regarded for those that have studied in the UK. It makes them feel they have a connection making business easier.

All visits are carefully planned, eating in restaurants not pubs and where possible we include an evening tour of a local village or historic building, nothing too grand or too long. At the factory, we can allocate a quiet office and put-up screens to make a prayer room if requested. These gestures are all welcomed and show respect. We always walk them around the factory, introducing them to the people that worked on their product or solution. I often introduce them to both my sister and nephew who work in the business because the UAE have the same strong family values. All this regional knowledge available on the internet and really helps relationships, it just shows you care and are putting effort in.

The first time we had customers from the UAE, I remember showing them their console for the first time. One look at their faces and I could see something was not right. What had I missed? They started asking, "Where is the mounting for this screen?"

"Where is the fitting for that box?" It was clear 25% of the equipment had not been allocated space. I showed them the list they provided me with from my first trip along with a copy of the design submitted in our proposal that was approved by them.

It did not take me long to work out the original parts list given to us was incorrect but how could I defend my business, so not to be blamed without making the person who gave me the list look incompetent? He was part of the visiting team and was looking uncomfortable Although they can all see that I have worked to the list provided, I announce, "It is a misunderstanding, of course, I thought this was 'THE' list but it is only a guide!"

"Must be our mistake. Let us work together now on how to correct this before it leaves the factory." I think I saved everyone from embarrassment but they were still unhappy for a while and blamed me but we got it all sorted in the end. Why did I not realise this was only a "guide"? I should have known there would be more equipment! There were times when it really was not easy working internationally!

The reason for international business was to give the company stability, so that if the UK was to go into a recession, another economy may be able to cover the shortfall. My tip is never to underestimate the time and money it takes to break into a new market/country, only take on one at a time and do your homework when you pick it.

Chapter Twenty-Seven
Fake News (Flagpoles and Fish tanks)

I just love this expression because it reminds of an old boss, who was also a good friend. His expression of 'Flagpoles and fish tanks' refers to the sort of items big corporates have in their reception areas that serve no purpose other than to look good or portray an image. A more modern term for the same thing is probably 'Fake News'.

He used it a lot because he wanted the sales guys to always make an assessment when they visited clients to see if they were credit worthy. He would want to know if the company had either money to burn, had taken their eye off the ball or had created a smoke screen to hide the truth. It is a difficult judgement to make because as a business gets bigger and more responsible, there are things as an owner you do that could suggest you are not focused on sales/growth and margins. Things linked to staff welfare, the environment or the community could fall into the 'flagpole and fish tank' area if you are not careful but there are still some clear warning signals you can take from a visit. Is the building quiet? Is the place run down? How full the car park is? To some companies how they look from the outside is not important so take that into account.

I remember a supplier coming to see me in the barn during the early days and I remember him giving me credit right away. I later asked him how he had come to that decision. He commented on how small the barn was but that it was full to bursting with product and he had to park far away because there were no spaces. Yes, the barn was run down but it was dry, well-lit and exactly what he expected to see from a busy small business. He also commented that he spotted the number of quotes I had on my desk and that he had to arrange a meeting as I would not let him just drop by because of how busy I was.

I remember reading a report from a recruiting company that the quality of the coffee at an office had a bearing on the quality of staff you could attract! I conducted a survey with my team and most of them could not give a toss but I went for a small upgrade anyway. I was always sure our welfare facilities were acceptable and clean. Perhaps the report was 'Fake News' and the recruiter also owned a coffee company! Who knows!

At one engineering firm, where I was commercial manager, I started interviewing for a new admin salesperson and all the applicants were women. It was a largely male workforce and the site was quite scruffy. The company only had two ladies working full time so we were thrilled that we had female applicants. One of the candidates after the interview asked if she could see the ladies toilet, which, of course, we showed her. They were fine, clean and tidy. She actually got the job and some months later, when we were working together, I asked her about the toilet check. She just said that it was important to her that the washrooms were clean and tidy. She did not care about the building or factory and could even bring a kettle if the tea machine was poor, but the toilet needed to be nice. I have always put effort into looking after people who choose to work for me, so it is good to know and recognise what is important and what makes them feel comfortable at work.

When we started visiting potential clients, we were on alert to check out how they were functioning. I would try and make an assessment as to whether the client was in a good financial position or not. It really helped me once in Switzerland when a company that had been around for 40 years called me for a project meeting. I had been trying to work with them for ages and finally they had a project for me to quote. Sounds great but I also needed to know why the sudden change of heart from their current suppliers. The building was quiet, the car park was empty. It was a big site but hardly anyone around. My gut told me there was an issue and I was correct. Within six months they had folded and we were thankful we had not given them any credit.

Always be focused. In the early days you have no choice because 'cash is king' and blowing your first decent month's money on a reception desk or a nice car just might not lead to more orders. There is a balance.! I remember a client in Qatar telling me once that I have a great product but I need to work on the wrapping. Interestingly, he said that the Chinese were completely opposite to the British in that their wrapping was fantastic but the product was rubbish. Read into that what you will.

The next time I had a VIP visit I put a lot more effort in at the barns and it worked. We had a big local authority visiting to inspect the first of several projects we were hoping to win. I had built up a friendship with Anne who worked for a small local authority body in Eastleigh (my borough council). She was really motivated and her role was to help small business and we got on really well. Once during a VIP visit she came down with a work colleague and they spent the day working on their laptops from my office. It made my office feel noisy and full. I had cleaned and painted where I could, to make the officers and workshop look good and it worked. Years later, the client told me he had been quite concerned when he first arrived but was re-assured when he saw lots of people busy and happy in their work! I have Anne to thank for that. In addition to that she did something else that really helped around a year later.

It gets harder now to spot what is fake. If you have a good website and the ability to photo-shop, it is amazing, what sort of image you can create company. I always check online to see how big a company is and get a credit approved rating. These things are difficult to disguise.

When I started, I could not afford to pay top money for staff and the offices and workshop were certainly basic. I had to talk people into joining with some direct honesty at the interview stage and dare I say it with my own motivation and charm. I am happy to say that we hardly lost a person we did not want to keep and now over 15 years later, we are regarded as a company that looks after its team well. Just remember, you can only pay what you can afford and if the person applying is not perfect, look at their potential and how you can develop them.

Back to Anne and how she helped me again. When the business was around a year old, I simply ran out of money. I had not paid myself for over a year, so had two full credit cards and was trying to work out how I could pay child support to my ex-wife. I was desperate, working all the hours, trying to win business. Anne popped over for a coffee and an update in her capacity as business support, and we talked it through. I told her I needed to try and sell an old car I had until the orders start to come in. I'm a petrol head. To start the business, I had to sell my motorbike, and now it was time for me to sell my 1970 Lotus. Anne told me that her husband was considering the purchase of a classic car and she would have a chat with him. 24 hours later, Anne and her husband, Martin, were standing looking at my car. I managed to get it started, but the car was not in any condition to drive. I talked through all the work I had done and confessed to the problems. He respected my honesty. Remember, I was quite desperate and a lot was hanging on this. Martin was in two minds which was fair. He walked around the car another time and turned to Anne and said, "OK, Anne, what do you think?"

She looked at him and replied, "I think it's one of the sexiest cars I've ever seen," before turning away and giving me a wink! A few days later, Martin organised the collection of the car. Three weeks later I picked up a decent order from a customer who paid up front and I was back in positive cash flow and back in business.

I will never forget the stress levels during that period and what Anne did for me. As a bonus, Martin and I also became mates, and for a period, played in a band together! The last time I talked to him he still had the car.

As I have said when you are looking at 'flag poles and fish tanks', it is sometimes difficult to work out the status of a firm. When my company was around six or seven years old, we were still not really making a lot of money. We were doing OK in that. Everyone was getting paid but there were so many things to invest in. This was a slow, expensive process because I wanted to pay cash for everything and not be tied to bank loans. It was frustrating because I thought the business was going well but everywhere I looked, there were other business owners driving nice cars and talking about their property portfolio when I was still driving around in my old van. I guess I was a bit envious of the success of the people around me. One afternoon, while having a cuppa with our accountant, also a close friend of mine, I talked about my frustration and how I could not work out why we were not doing as well. I do not think he realised at the time but he gave me the motivational speech I needed. He held up my accounts and said, "Look, Wayne, this is all built from scratch. It is a journey; the numbers do not lie. You are doing well, so keep going. Everything you said you wanted to do you are doing, perhaps, not as fast as you want, but you are profitable and you are watching the right things. The cash flow and bank balance is all good."

I asked him about how others were more successful and highlighted a guy we both knew in particular. Graham's answer was, "It's a house of cards, Wayne, all smoke and mirrors." Fake news.

When you run a company, it is sometimes difficult to know if you are doing the right thing. I was not born a managing director. You may read stories of how a 21-year-old has grown a firm more or less overnight and is now worth millions but the reality is this person is the exception not the rule.

The internet has created the phenomenon of 'Fake News' and that is what this is all about. It is merely propaganda in a different format (remember the coffee machine question). My generation are far more trusting and perhaps less tolerant, so the young people reading this will be much better at spotting what my generation would call 'flag poles and fish tanks'. The great thing about the internet, however, is it works both ways. In that, you can find out so much about people and business. There is so much personal information out there if you look for it, so use it to find the truth.

Chapter Twenty-Eight
No Money, No Honey

This expression was said to me by a Scandinavian guy, quite recently, in Saudi Arabia of all places.

I was in a meeting with him and three of his team and we were discussing payment terms for a project. My biggest tip I could ever give is to talk money as early as you can, and if you have any doubts, do not give credit.

This was a prime example of working with international companies across borders makes it hard to debt chase, so really make sure you have control of either the goods or the money all the way through the project. I knew this was a problem client, so insisted that stage payments were made before we started manufacturing. They slipped on all of them and the final release of cash was due before the goods left my factory. They were now insisting the goods must be in SA before they would release the final payment because of local law! This was complete tosh and I was having none of it. Later that day, we were attending site with the end client (an extremely important customer), who wanted to talk to me about project delays. I apologised saying the project was very technical. I did not want to drop my customer in it and advised that I was resolving things internally. I later discovered the client knew exactly what was going on because dozens of items had not arrived, not just ours and it was all down to payment.

Negotiation on payment terms is difficult as a salesperson. You work so hard to win business and the last thing you want is so to introduce a barrier to the sale, but what is the point of doing it if you do not get paid! Your employees will still expect to be paid along with everyone else even if you're not.

The four people kept me at the table during this particular meeting for a further 90 minutes, telling me to release the goods. Even when I showed them their payment history, which was terrible, they just blamed admin and us for the delays. Eventually, they did pay and when our engineers arrived on site, they could not start work because the suspended floor had not been installed to stand our equipment on because the contractors had not been paid by our client. They clearly had run out of money. Our engineers were delayed three days waiting for the work to be completed and by then, the end user was involved. Even then, we were limited in what we could do because of other contractors on site doing their delayed work. The client begged us to stay. I sent them a quote. They did not pay it, so our engineers came home. It was completely brutal, the client was so angry with me but if they had paid their invoices on time, then they would not have put themselves in this situation! No money, no honey was the expression they joked with me the first time I met them, but they were right.

Never be afraid to talk about money to a client, make it clear what the costs are and the stages of payment. What is the point in spending days trying to sell someone a Rolex when all they have the budget for is a Timex?

Interestingly, this can lead onto your market positioning and your marketing plan. If you are constantly talking to people who cannot afford you, then something is wrong. You must point your business and efforts at your target market.

Talk to your customers. Most of the time a client does not want you to go out of business. Be aware of the work you are trying to win and make sure you can fund it. What I mean by this expression is if the project is a million pounds and you need to spend £750k before you get paid, make sure you plan for it and can afford the up-front costs. This is what my client failed to do. The project was huge and they could not afford to run it.

As a relatively new company, be aware of winning a big project. If you have a relatively short history in business, why would a contract of that size be awarded to you? Perhaps you are just brilliant and all your competitors had an off day but do your due diligence and check, it is not too good to be true.

With another good size project in the Middle-East and probably one of our largest we gave no credit but we did allow some flexibility with staged payments. Everything went fine and during the work we were surprised to see a new company being used on one of the products. Unfortunately, they were a classic case of being too keen too soon. This was big project which they had under-priced and they then found themselves being hung out to dry over payment terms. The company went bust and their equipment did not even get turned on! We were back on site a year later, modifying our equipment to fit the new supplier. I don't think some of these big contractors even realise the stress and worry they put on people when they do not pay and that livelihoods can be ruined.

We have been caught out three or four times over the last 20 years. It is a good idea to make provision in your accounts for a bad debt as it's called. Even if you agree everything in advance, sometimes people choose what they want to hear or just ignore your plans.

So, some tips when it comes to money. Never be afraid to talk about it and if you can, agree terms before you fully commit. Your first position is payment with order, then go from there. Staged payments with all or most of the money before you release the goods is a place you want to be at. Think about what are you going to do if they do not pay?

We have a late payment fee in our terms of contract, but I have never enforced this and do not know any companies who have. We have a series of letters that we can use before engaging a debt collection company to send a letter. In the UK this is often enough. We have agreed a fixed fee for each letter and budget for this during the year. You have the ability to take clients to court. In the UK you have a chance for sure but internationally, you will spend a lot on legal fees and in reality not get very far.

Another option is to factor the debt. This is like selling the debt to a business (usually a bank) who will pay you in advance of the money arriving for a percentage fee. This can work for some companies but can be a slippery slope and expensive to get out of. It also removes valuable margin from your bottom line. Get advice from a couple of sources before going down this route.

Another tip I did learn was a rule of three as a friend called it. When quoting, I would give the client three options. A luxury high end design, which was expensive, a middle of the road design with equivalent costs and a budget design with low costs, only providing the basics. There are lots of studies that show when a customer gets three options. They go for the middle one as they want value but do not necessarily want cheap. I would then do the same with payment terms. If they paid up front, they got a discount, payment on deliver was the quoted price and if credit was given, it would cost more.

Don't be a busy fool. You have to get paid for what you do.

Chapter Twenty-Nine
Lonely Game

So, you decide to go out on your own and start a business. Remember those first few words because sometimes it is going to feel like you are literally out on your own. In the early days and even now, there are times when I personally feel completely alone when it comes to running the business and making the bigger decisions. Nowadays we are more mindful of stress, mental illness and depression. It is very important that as a person and business owner, you manage to keep things in check on how you are coping. I am fascinated to see my friends asking each other about their health mentally and physically. As a man in his 50s, I am a bit from the 'toughen up and get on with it' generation.

From the outside looking in, it must be difficult for others to see the pressure business can put on us. I have a nice house and a nice car. I have two holidays a year so everything is Rosie, right! Not completely, I have never really managed to cope with stress but I am aware of it and lucky for me I found a way to switch off. I discovered sailing and for the last ten years have been trying to work out how to do it without endangering myself or others! Interestingly, I enjoy some of the risks and challenges (and the stress) of offshore racing. I am fully aware that I am not the best sailor and definitely not a natural. It took me over a year to get over seasickness! But because of the concentration levels and effort, I must put in. I forget about the business while I am out there. Perhaps, I have swapped one type of stress for another! Blimey, work that one out.

I did have some preparation for working alone. I spent many years as a traditional sales representative driving up and down the country. As a field salesperson, you have to be a socially comfortable person within a group, then happy in a one to one and also able to travel for long periods by yourself. As I got better at sales, I actually spent more time alone because the travel time got much longer between meetings. Flights to Dubai and the UAE became a monthly trip. I think this time alone really developed me as a person, having to be self-reliant but also keen to maximise my time while away.

I can still remember some of my first flights alone, not sleeping the night before and getting to the airport hours early, then on arrival, worrying about getting a taxi (I got ripped off a few times). Uber is a revelation by the way!

From an owner's perspective, your levels of loneliness change as often as the tide comes in and out. You must lead and try to set an example. Your mission is to act as you would like others to act, setting an example for others. This gets easier and as you introduce more processes, people get a feel for what 'good looks like'. At Thinking Space, we have clear values and we can follow them through 100% with the actions we take. This then in theory spreads the standards around the business. Interestingly, as these processes evolve and the work becomes a little more corporate, the loneliness eases because others know your objective and the overall aim.

Have no misconceptions about being at the top of the tree. There is only room for one, even PLC companies need a top person driving things along with a board and good team but the buck literally stops with you. The roll of making final decision has never been difficult for me but as a person with a sales background, I have always worried about where the next sale is coming from. I constantly look at ways to make the product easier to sell. Try to maintain that customer focus and listen in order to give them what they want.

In the early days, I struggled to find people in the same position as me. Some of the networking groups I worked my way around were too small, people that were happy to be one-person bands or worked on the side of a main income and that was not my plan. I remember joining a business link scheme called PLATO. This was part of a government quango called Business Link. It was free and designed for business owners who wanted to grow. For me there is nothing better than learning from people who have been there, seen it and done it, so to spend time with likeminded owners was priceless. It was like having a board of directors on your shoulder who wanted to help and be helped. They understood the pressure that's linked to needing to win work to pay your mortgage. Every month we would get together and talk. Sometimes we would arrange a guest speaker.

The group was good for me. They gave me some degree of confidence but also pointed me in the direction of good value business coaches. Do not underestimate the value of training, learning and taking advice from others.

Remember, you do not need to follow it, the decision is yours what you do with the information.

When I sailed across the Atlantic, there were times when I would do a solo watch to give the crew longer to rest and sleep. These solo watches were really good for me and during those periods I sort of 'found myself'. I had moments when I missed my children so much but then had moments where the usual stresses and worries were completely gone. We had no phones or outside contact for two weeks and I think all of us were better for it. Strangely for me, the time flew too quickly in the end. I did not miss my usual daily interaction with different people. The crew were all I needed and the solitude for periods was great. The trip taught me that being lonely is not necessarily about being alone.

Another tip from me is to find a few friends or businesspeople, who have truly been in the same position as you. We all experience things differently but the fact that you can talk to someone who has possibly been stood in the same place as you can really help. I had a period in the early days when I thought I was going to end up out of work with a debt of £25k. Of course, there was also the indignity of failing. Unless someone has been close to that position, they cannot contemplate the pressure, the stress or loneliness. On the plus side, you do get used to it. I have definitely learnt from it and cope quite well. Now, to be fair, my hair is very grey. I wonder if that is connected.

There are also some other things that I now do to keep me connected, grounded and stress free. To start with I get out and about, I go down to my little boat and even if I don't sail, I have a little 'tinker'. I will clean something, sit outside, breathe the air and deliberately do very little, no timelines, no pressure. For me, feeling good can really help. I try and have a healthy diet and exercise when I can. This is not easy when you are working for yourself because making time is not so easy. I joined a gym with tennis facilities. I deliberately never played league matches but I did arrange games against new friends I met. Try to have something outside of work to focus on that perhaps does not carry too much responsibility. I also love a bit of retail therapy, I am not talking online shopping but walking around the malls, talking to salespeople and picking clothes that make you feel nice. My family is important and it is easy to neglect them when you are always working, time with my children is precious and they are a great help in relieving the stresses of work.

Try to get a life outside of work. I know this sounds simple but if you are buried in work as owners, often our relationships will suffer for sure. This includes your family and your friends, so be aware of it and give them time. Stay positive and surround yourself with others that are positive and remember to do what you can to avoid the lonely game.

Chapter Thirty
Pass the Parcel

When I started out, it was only the first year when I did 'everything' on my own. The little business plan I had written had to include employees as a manufacturer of products. The only other choice would have been to buy components in and I did not want that. As I mentioned earlier, Paul Atkins joined me as a shareholder but with me having the major share options. This was because I knew that further down the road I might need to distribute more shares.

The business has completely changed now. I found that hard to adjust to but do understand the need for change and you should too. The business will evolve and will grow. Our change was to get the sales and marketing much more focused on the products and services that were most profitable for us.

The development of processes within a business can be painful but its benefits are tenfold. I have talked to owners, who see admin as a medium that slows things down and at the start, I would suggest that was the feeling I had but as we grew it was vital. With a team of sales guys and a group of designers and fitters, there must be clear information transfer, otherwise you will end up chasing your tail and make mistakes. The introduction of good admin processes frees up people. They can work remotely and over different hours.

One of my pet hates is the micromanager. Being able to 'pass the parcel' or pass the responsibility is vital to growth. If you constantly get involved with everything someone does, the company will only manage to grow to within your own work capacity. The knock-on from this is, when you sell the business, it is not worth as much, because you do not have the processes in place and when you leave, the firm is worth less because it cannot function without you.

Fortunately, for me, I knew from the start that one of my weaknesses was that I struggled with detail. That lack of detail meant I had to delegate some of the project work from the beginning because I would either forget it or not actually ask the correct questions in the first place. Even now I know some of the team dread a handover from me! I try every day to be more accurate, following the processes we have written can only help with that.

It is so important to embrace the changes within the business and to delegate well. I always start with what I want the outcome to be or 'what does good look like'. By stating the goal or clear outcome, it gives the person you are delegating to, scope to do something their way rather than your way, but that will achieve the same objective. They might even do it better then you.

Just remember, this all helps productivity, time management, and moral. It helps people to learn and gain credibility and confidence. All of this can only help the bottom line.

The idea of passing the parcel goes much further than just delegation. It has to be part of the growth and development of you and your business. For example, my role within the business recently changed from managing director to CEO/Chairman. I am now only seeing the performance of the business in an overview every three months. This decision was part of the plan for growth, but tough for me personally to cope with. I cannot tell you how we are doing until I get the numbers from the directors because I have delegated this work to them. The point is, it stops me dipping in and making changes that are not planned. It is very difficult to make a transition from being hands-on to hands-off, but to achieve the growth we want, this has to happen.

My role now is about what the business will look like in a years' time and what new products, services and acquisitions, we will bring in to achieve our growth targets. It is a massive change for me and changes the dynamic. We are trying to empower the managers more (passing the parcel to them) giving them clear goals and objectives that change as the business changes. I in turn have a different parcel to manage.

The final thing I would add is, never let a manager hang on to a responsibility or hold it exclusively. I have heard stories where people think that if they are the only ones to know something, then their job is safe. That is just not true. Try not to allow that situation to arise and aim to develop a culture of knowledge sharing. Some people think they won't get credit if they share the work and others might feel if they share the workload they are showing they can't cope. Work hard to promote teamwork and a culture that is better than that.

I am not going to go into any more detail regarding delegation. There are already lots of books on it, so I will hand over that responsibility to you. See what I have done there? Yes, delegated!

Chapter Thirty-One
The Rocking Chair

As the leader, you need to have a clear vision of the goal or end game and, of course, keep moving the goal forward. From that point, you will be communicating with your managers, who in turn pass this down the line to the various team members. That's your focus and all standard managerial stuff, but this chapter is not about the things you should be focusing on but more about the things you should not, especially if you cannot influence them.

If you are sat in a rocking chair, enjoy the chair and do not worry about its function or rocking motion. Do not think about how it rocks, how it moves or the radius of the rails, just accept it.

As a business owner and once you have a team in place, you must do the same. Do not worry about the small details that has to be someone else's responsibility. You do need to manage things that matter or check these things are being managed by one of your team, but remember, your role in the bigger picture. This is not easy, but it is all part of the process of handing over responsibility and if you can work out what is important and what is not, you will be able to relax and enjoy things more. As the business grows, this is vital, but even when you start out, knowing what the true priorities will keep you focused on things you need to do today.

The rocking chair analogy is also about trying not to worry about things you cannot influence. You can react to changes and as you become more experienced, you will learn to see the need for change both more clearly and earlier. I am a bit of a worrier, so every day I have to remind myself of where I am, how I feel and the how those feelings are received by others. I remember my sister telling me one night what a miserable old man I had become. I was devastated by her comments, but she was right, and now I work hard to remind myself how privileged and lucky I am and try not to sweat the small stuff. The world around

COVID-19 has affected a lot of people in a negative way, as an employer in any major situation like this you need to prioritise and work out the important actions to take, such as keeping people safe and making sure the business can function so that everyone can still get paid. Protecting the company so it can function in the future and controlling costs are all things you need to focus on. We worked together to keep each other safe physically, but I deliberately spent time working on the mental state of our staff.

It was a surprise how the situation affected people so differently and how some of the younger team members were more upset by it than others. Our managers have invested a lot of time in understanding how to recognise mental illness and discussing stress related illness with everyone within the business. Personally, I found that giving people your time and reassuring them about the state of the business helped, mainly people wanted job security reassurance. What I could not afford to worry about was the virus itself, the state of the economy, Brexit or the global reaction etc. This was the message I passed to everyone because it was something we cannot control. I remember actively making sure the facts and our responsibilities were clear and worked hard to encourage people not to believe everything published on social media.

Try not to worry about the past either, believe me I have made some massive mistakes in business and in my private life. Do not worry what others think and gossip. I would never attend an exhibition because of fear of what the industry thought. I would attend because it is good for the company. People will always have an opinion and you have already worked out that not everyone loves you (you are not pizza).

Another thing you have no control over is getting old. I have gone grey and bits of me ache, but enjoy the journey, embrace it and make the most of your time, remember to 'smell the roses'. Never worry about making a mistake, it is how we learn and improve. Be ready to hold your hands up but do not dwell too much on it, move on because you will make another one at some point, nobody is perfect. Remember these things when you judge your team as well.

The next thing to not worry about is the price tag. This can be the price you pay for things, so just get value for money and make sure the margin is there but more importantly always defend the price you sell your product for, it is that price because it is worth it.

Work on not worrying about things that cannot be influenced but also work on the indicators that show the signs of stress in yourself. Always try to cut yourself some slack and remind yourself that you are not invincible and try to find a person you can confide in.

Remember to focus on the bigger picture and the future. Over the years I have lost what I thought were key members of staff but we are still here and every now and again someone joins, and they turn out to be an absolute gem. Sometimes, you just cannot pay enough to keep people or personal circumstances change, such as the person wanting to get into something we cannot offer. I am a firm believer in training and personally have found it keeps people with you longer. The training and development of your team should be part of your culture and the company's DNA. Sometimes it is restricted by time or budgets, however, if you look around, you can get some good training that is not too expensive and often staff will commit some of their own time to develop their careers. There is a bit of planning required and efforts should be made to map a career path rather than just selecting random courses but this can be discussed if you work together.

There are a few things you can do that will help you to stop worrying. Try to come to terms with the fact that it is OK not to be completely in control and that nobody is perfect. Try to always cut yourself a little slack. One thing that has always worked for me is exercise, some running seems to give me time to put the world to rights and also my sailing helps.

Learn from mistakes, don't dwell on them and if you can build a good team, problems can be solved easier together. Remember the rocking chair and do not over think.

Chapter Thirty-Two
Kill with Kindness

This expression was said to me when working in North America. Our US agent, Kevin, was having a hard time with a client and he was telling me all about it. With a smile on his face, he said that all we had to do was kill him with kindness. I really liked the expression. It is a way of getting in control and realising you need to perhaps step back and review the situation and just be kind.

A couple of years later, I saw him use it in anger. He flew over to the UK for a meeting with me and the team to discuss the installation of a project that he was going back to do later in the month. The client was screaming for delivery and for him to attend site as soon as he returned home. Because we were so busy at the time, he agreed to run the site work himself, so a planning meeting was needed with some training.

We talked while driving back from the airport where I collected him. He was keen to see where in the world the crate was so he could confirm to the client it was on route but he was having trouble getting the tracking details. You can imagine his surprise when we got the factory and the goods were only just being packed for shipping. That is why there was no tracking data! I did not know if he was going to explode, freak out or have a heart attack! In fact, he looked at Paul our operations director, shook his hand and said how fantastic it looked, he killed us with kindness. Of course, he then went on to mention the pain we were going to go through together when telling the customer the goods had not yet left. Kevin took photos and the next morning the packed cases were on a truck to the airport. He then called the customer.

Kevin could have complained and quite rightly so, but in his situation, what would complaining have done? The products were being packed and the trucks were arriving. The work had been done, not as quickly as he had wanted but the product looked good. All he and we could do was communicate this to the customer. I learnt a lot from him as we had dinner that night talking about it.

It is so easy to complain. In some instances, it must be done, however, finding a solution is more important. Even when you do complain, make sure you know what you want from it.

I spent a year trying to negotiate a new lease with our managing agent. During a time of COVID-19 and a pending recession, we were being asked for a new contract that was 40% more than the previous deal. The agent and I were at loggerheads during our negotiations and there had been some very heated phone calls and emails. Our relationship was not good. Finally, one day during an exchange of emails, he suggested we simply moved out! I had clearly pushed him too far. Some research and investigation on my part showed that my previous deal had been very good and that there was a massive shortage of industrial buildings. What I had failed to do was kill the agent with kindness. I kept the communication moving and then offered to hand the negotiations over to a colleague. If you do get to a point where you have burnt your bridges, then hand the discussion over to someone else. I am not sure the kindness strategy would have worked here but there was certainly no reason for me to get quite so animated.

When you put everything into your work, it is very easy to and quite natural to be protective of it. Try to always take stock and remove any emotion in business. Always remember it is not personal if you can. I have fallen out with suppliers and some potential customers over the way they have worked with us. It is really difficult in business because you cannot always choose who you work with. We have a local business that has always been a challenge to communicate with. As a company they are at the lower end of the spectrum in the market they are in but they do have a good active marketing department and win a lot of business on price. In fact, they win so much work. We are constantly trying to become their preferred supplier. With so much emphasis on cutting cost, it is a fine balancing act because as a company we are aiming at the premium end. This does not make us a better business or them a lesser one. It just means we are focusing on different sectors of the market. This makes working together more of a challenge but because they are local, some saving could be made with communication and transportation. What we discovered was that their attempts to keep costs low actually devalued our product. Often we would find ourselves lacking information to complete the quality solution that we built our brand on.

It is important once you have positioned your product in the market that you strive to maintain it. Since then a new CEO has been appointed at the company. They have the drive to lift the quality and relationship with the contractors, so we are slowly winning more business because the positioning of the two companies is more aligned.

If there is any advice in the book you should really take on board, it is the concept of 'not burning your bridges'.

Try to balance your approach against what the future relationship could look like. Remember, those you are in conflict with, could be future customers, suppliers or employees, you just never know!

Always try to calm down and give yourself a moment. See if you can identify the core of the problem and then see if you can fix it rather than sending a sweeping angry email.

If you find yourself in conflict, try to end it as soon as you can. If these drag out and fester, they tend to get worse. Remember, in business, you have competitors not enemies.

A successful conclusion or ending in hostilities requires the participation of not only those who are involved with the original agreement but also others around you, sometimes a good tip is to use someone to mediate.

There are also advantages to being kind. It supposedly releases good hormones. In addition, being kind eases your own stress and anxiety, possibly helping you live longer! It must be worth a try.

When my children were still as school, I challenged them each day to try to carry out a 'random act of kindness' (RAK). When they read this, I will see if they remember. What I regard as a RAK is doing something kind for a stranger. I am not talking about doing something you should already do like open a door for someone but, for example, recently, while at lunch with a friend, when I went to pay, I also paid the bill of the table next to me where two elderly ladies were sat. I did not tell them. I just talked to the manager of the restaurant to sort things out and then left. I could not tell you who they were or what they looked like but that was the point, it was random.

A couple of years ago, I accidently hit a traffic cone while driving on a horrible wet day and it got stuck under my car making a terrible noise as it scraped along the road. I pulled into a layby only to find it was jammed solid deep under the engine bay. My problem was I was wearing a suit. Suddenly, a young guy appeared who was wearing Hi-Viz clothing and dressed for outdoor work. He must have seen me struggling to work out how to get under the car without getting dirty and as he said, "I will sort that for you." He crawled under the car and pulled out the cone. He was covered in dirty water from the road. I did not know what to do. I offered to go to the garage and get him a coffee but he just said,

"No, thanks." So all I could do was thank him very much for his help. That was a great 'random act of kindness' and one I will never forget.

I have a friend who works for the Samaritans as a volunteer. I have so much respect for her. It is a job I do not think I would be any good at. She said that sometimes people need to be told that they are doing OK and that they are a nice person. When you are at work and managing people, try to manage the way you communicate. As a business owner, you can be quite formidable.

Just remember you are the person responsible for your own actions. In life and as a business owner, there is nowhere to hide because it is your actions that define you. I was once told to try and reach a resolution where everyone wins when in conflict or perhaps get to a compromise where the other person feels like they have won. If you can, why not, as long as you get what you need.

If you do unintentionally burn a bridge, then own up to the mistake and apologise for the conflict. Be specific so it is kept in isolation and do your best to keep things in context and do not dwell on issues. The main thing is to at least try, it is difficult to argue with kindness.

The final note from me is to try to communicate in person. In a virtual world people can become keyboard warriors but face to face takes a different courage and when you actually see the affect and tone of someone's response and body language, things can tend to be easier to resolve.

If it fails, go to whatever plan B is? I do not have endless plans but I do often need to modify the current plan if things go wrong. Perhaps, just kill with kindness in the first place. This is the most often used expression we use within our companies.

Chapter Thirty-Three
Fire in Your Belly

"Wayne, you have always had fire in your belly," was an expression a friend said to me once. I am a person that needs a goal, a challenge or a mountain to climb. I have found this not just in business but also outside work and I am not alone. Setting small, short terms objectives that build up around your longer, bigger plans is an easy management tool to use with your teams. There are a lot of books available about this and 'SMART' objectives that follow these principles. I think they work and have not changed as a process really for 20 years.

But there are other attributes that I have as a person that sort of highlight not only my personality but that of a standard entrepreneur. We are not perfect beasts, apparently, (who knew!) but none of us are and if we understand our weaknesses, we can work on them and employee people that can fill the gaps. There are many ways to work out your traits and perhaps areas you are weak in, quite often just experience will tell you but I would always recommend a psychometric testing method. They are not necessarily 100% accurate, but they do paint a good picture of yourself and your team. For me, they give you a bit of an indication of your style. It does not mean you are bad in any way, but it makes you more aware. If your managers also do the same and share the data, suddenly it feels like you have an insight into how people like to work.

I did not really go in for psychology until a colleague talked me into running a Belbin behavioural and psychometric test for the management team (there are loads of others also available). It was a revelation. I will not detail individual results, but I can share one thing with you. When I first assembled the management team in the early days, I could not work out why some of the team were more vocal in meetings than others. I could not understand why one of the managers was so disengaged during the meeting itself. We had known each other for many years and I knew he was on board and motivated. The Belbin test gave me the answer.

The test reports a lot of things, but one thing it did highlight was the manager in question craved detail. He wanted to understand fully what was going to be discussed before he would commit or comment. He needed information in advance and could not 'shoot from the hip' because it was not his nature. This information was gold to me. In business, we need a mix of qualities. I am not a details person, so I am fully aware of the sort of businesspeople I need to surround myself with. My tip for you is to try and get a mix of skills in your business.

Remember the rules about nurture and not nature, people can learn and develop skills, so the tests also give you opportunity to set up programs to develop people.

In my opinion, a business owner and an entrepreneur are two different things. There are lots of people who can take a company, grow it by developing good processes and perhaps careful recruitment. Lots of accountants are good business owners, but realistically by nature, they are numbers people and perhaps not big risk takers. Think about it, the last thing we want is our accountant to be a bit of a gambler! This is a good thing by the way, my company is now established and with nearly 20 years of growth, it now has a systems and process person about to head it up.

The trouble is, I am not that type of person. I am about to break away and start something new. I want to gamble and grow and this is the difference. Some would say I am not contented and perhaps that is a trait of an entrepreneur, always looking for the next mountain to climb. Believe me when I say I do really hope that one day I sit back and enjoy my lot but right now I still want to take over the world and the global pandemic has only highlighted it

If you are truly driven, do not apologise for it but be aware of it. I always try to behave in a more charismatic way rather than using a blunt focused approach. We can all improve our communication skills and if we keep the passion and enthusiasm alive, then it can really help teamwork. I always focus on positive things with other people around and do have some level of self-confidence. If you earn respect and build it over time, then there is a good chance you will have these traits too.

I am a person who likes to learn from those who have been there and done it. I get a lot more out of talking to an owner, who like me was gambling with his house when making decisions and not following a manual or spreadsheet. I have completed a lot of training courses but one weeks residential course was unforgettable.

The training was Field Sales and we had been on site at a country hotel for four days with the final morning being a series of tests and presentations. On the eve of the final day, we were tasked to produce a training video. During the week the sales guys had got to know each other and were of course sharing war stories and one guy told us about what is probably an urban myth but is worth telling because of its later consequences. It goes something like:

A guy attends an interview for a sales role in a small company. The interview does not go well and it is clear the owner does not think highly of candidate applying for the role and is quite damming . The candidate knows it is not the job he wants and is just waiting to leave when the owner says, "Look, if you are a good sales guy, then sell me this glass of water on the table." This question is the final straw for the candidate but he thinks on his feet, he reaches into his pocket and takes out a box of matches. He opens the box, lights all of them and with a flick of the wrist throws the now lit box into the waste bin beside them. It is full of paper, so quickly ignites. The boss looks at him in shock and while the room starts to fill with smoke, he makes eye contact the candidate who says, "Want to buy a glass of water?"

Off we went in small groups to create our training videos. One of the group still had that crazy story ringing in their ears and decided to re-create it. The next thing we know, the fire alarms are ringing and we are heading out to the car park to our designated muster point, where we got a full run down of events from the group in question. The bin apparently was too full of paper and the smoke alarms signalled a full hotel evacuation! If you are going to go big, I suggest you plan ahead!

Entrepreneurs constantly try to test themselves. I doubt the decisions I take every day while always trying to demonstrate a strong sense of self on the outside. It is only in later years I have been able to confess this to my fellow directors and it is a credit to both of them that they help me cope with the levels of doubt and self-inflicted stress that creates.

Like most entrepreneurs, there is also a level of passion, creativity and resilience that are common features. But this all goes hand in hand with a lot of mistakes because of the lack of detail and the willingness to take risk.

It all sounds very cool but there are fine lines where perhaps a successfully entrepreneur could be considered aggressive or narcissistic and sometimes a little too ruthless. I wonder if someone like Elon Musk would consider himself to have some of these traits. He has taken great risks despite his wealth and doesn't feel the need to show how driven he is because the world can see it. I am sure he has levels of irresponsibility but I must say I would also suggest he has definitely done more good than harm. Classic leaders do have a bit of an issue with authority. I, for one, hate all the red tape and bureaucracy but perhaps this is linked to my dislike of detail as well.

If we look at the extreme end of the scale, we are talking about 'Wolf of Wall Street' characters, who have high social skills combined with low moral inhibitions. This combination can get you and your friends into a lot of trouble, to the point where you perhaps use manipulation for personal gain. I do not know anybody in business like this because I would suggest they would not last long and get worked out soon enough.

With 'fire in your belly' you can achieve a lot; you just need to control it. If you are not perfect, try to remember the people around you are not either and cut them some slack. The fire within drives you and it can make you quick to criticise so be conscious of that.

Finally, I would also say that the risks I have taken have been somewhat calculated. I am not a maniac and not the best role model either, that is probably my only thing in common with Elon, who I have to admit has been a little more successful than me!

Chapter Thirty-Four
Leave Nothing on the Table

It is easy to get dragged into a race to the bottom when you need sales. What I mean by this is because you are desperate for work, selling things for low margins could appeal. As you have read previously, keeping cash flow going is vital and there is some merit in keeping things ticking over but be mindful that you are here to make money, so plan how you can slowly grow your margin.

It is how we did it and I am sure it is not unusual as a business grows for the prices to increase. As we got bigger and better, we invested in product development, we relocated to nicer buildings and started to pay ourselves more. Of course, this means we needed to make more money. I am not going to talk about increasing your profit here but as you grow, your reputation builds and that has value to the customer, which gives you the opportunity to charge more. Economies of scale come into play regarding your buying power and your processes start to increase efficiency, therefore, helping profits.

This chapter is more about the external relationship rather than your internal efforts to make more margin. We are going to talk about insuring you have left 'nothing on the table'. I picked this expression up from a competitor at a trade show. I always try to maintain a level of respect and contact with all my competitors. Remember these people are the competition, not the enemy. The business owner congratulated me on winning a project he had also bid for (through gritted teeth) but did say I had undercut him and left 'money on the table'. This expression relates to the client's budget. The customer had more to spend, so why did I not take it!

This sounds a little aggressive and perhaps unethical to charge more but let me put this into context. If you can find out the budget a client has, you can save time by providing something that is right for them. Time saved, then saves money and the customer gets better value and more product for the known budget. It fascinates me the reluctance of people to tell you what their budget is. I assume this is because you have not built up a level of trust. Does the customer think that you will charge them £10 or even more if they have told you their budget is £10 regardless of how much it cost to make? If you could offer them an £8, £10 or £12 product and you know their budget is £10 then you have cracked it, as you know what they can afford and you can give them options.

If you do not listen to the customer or do not believe them, then how can you develop trust? People buy from people and brands they trust. Last year my partner wanted to change her car as it was starting to show its age. It was a small Mercedes convertible and she loved it, so shopping around was easy because she just wanted another one. The plan was to go to the main dealer first, then just nip over to another brand for a price comparison before she signed on the dotted line. We arrived at the Mercedes dealership, sat down with the sales guy and looked at the cars while drinking a posh coffee. We had a budget for monthly repayments and we wanted a second-hand car which we would own at the end. We were there for three hours while the sales guy kept showing us deals we could not afford, deals where the monthly fee was OK but we had to return the car in three years or make a large balloon payment at the end. All the deals were on new cars. In the end we walked out vowing never to go back there. There was no trust! That afternoon we also visited an Audi dealer, more posh coffee and a very young sales guy sat us down and asked us what we wanted. Of course, he was given the Mercedes story!

He took everything we told him on board. He then showed us a car which we liked which came within budget, so we ended up buying it there and then. It still disappoints me today that the first sales guy had a focus on selling us a new car. When we went to pick up the Audi, I talked about this with the sales manager. His opinion was that they probably did not have a car we wanted in stock but what they did have was a new car arriving which they needed to sell, so instead of giving us what we wanted, he was trying to sell us what he had. We spent our budget with the second garage and of course they now get to service the car regularly and do any maintenance.

There is a level of psychology here. If you are buying, you will probably have a little more money to spend than you tell the sales guy and let's be honest, if you are shown something close to the budget and perhaps a little better, then you might well go for it.

We are in business to not only make money but to provide products and services to our customers. If we want them to come back and recommend us to others, then we need to look after them. Looking after the customer especially in the longer term can also add to your bottom line which is a win for everyone. 'Leaving nothing on the table' is not just about selling your product at the maximum price the client is willing to pay. We are talking about the long-term support. If we can take away the pain regarding the follow-on services, we can offer, then we have the opportunity to 'up sell'.

It is an American sounding term but 'up selling' is what a sales assistant is trying to do to you when they offer you a polish to go with your shoes or when you buy a car and the person tries to sell you insurance, added warranty or a special coating that keeps the car clean! These are all efforts to up-sell to you. 'Leaving nothing on the table' is the same expression but perhaps more direct because everything on the table is up for grabs and you want it!

I am often amazed that at the start of negotiations, a customer will push hard on price, stating that they don't have the budget, so we give them a great deal and at the last moment they add a list of additional items, which they somehow find the money for, along with the additional charges for a faster delivery. This demonstrates that there is still often something on the table.

More generally, from a sales and marketing function, make sure it is part of your plan and the tone is right. To be more specific, try not to sound desperate to sell. If you do have a limited stock or time period to sell, then of course that can be used with a tone change. In these instances, you can introduce some urgency. In the past I have called clients to let them know about potential long lead times or future price increases to give them an option to buy now but you have to mean it and tell the truth.

An approach I really like is to demonstrate proof of an offer or option. If you can make savings if the customer buys now, then let them know what the saving is and if you can provide proof that the saving is genuine, then great. I remember an estate agent showing me around a house when looking for my first home. He told me if I wanted it I should get an offer to him right away. I did not believe him as I thought he was just pushing for a sale but when I called him the next day, the property had already sold. I was disappointed, he simply said that he had warned me but what he did not do was provide the reason why. He was so smug and I remembered that and did not use him again. He lost my trust and even though he was correct, his approach put me off using him again.

When does 'leaving nothing on the table' finish and a complete new order begin? In my opinion they are linked until the invoice is paid. Keep in touch via email and through social media and if you do this, then the client relationship will grow. If they are happy and you get no more business, the minimum you can be assured of is they are probably not going anywhere else. In addition, they might recommend you and that is a new 'table' of opportunity altogether.

Always combine the customer journey with the sales function and products within the business. We always keep a record of our sales and know when each item sold is ready for replacement or upgrade. This helps us launch upgrades and gives us an indication when a product is due for change or comes to the end of its life. Pretty basic marketing but looking after existing clients is one great way to keep getting access to their table!

Whatever your offer is, be sure you stay true to the product or brand message. One of my biggest customers last year used us several times to source small value items that were not in our standard range. On one occasion, they sent a shopping list from their customer that included web links to stools, ladders and cupboards amongst other items that they wanted us to provide. We contacted all the suppliers, got the lead times and then marked up the prices before sending over the quote. I would not regard this as standard up-selling but as it was linked to a previous project and the total value was high, I did it. It proved to be a nightmare. We did not get to select the suppliers because they were picked by the client. When we placed the orders, everything had to be paid for before delivery and our client was on a 90-day payment term. In addition, we had to deliver all the goods together in one shipment and one item was on an eight week lead time. This type of work costs money but a customer is not always going to see that, so be careful what additional products you agree to supply. In an effort to help the customer, I felt like it did not do our relationship any good because we could not control the quality of the products or the delivery times. It was not part of our plan!

Leaving nothing on the table takes skill but remember why you are working so hard. To make money.

Chapter Thirty-Five
Lucky Boy

This book is all about me giving it to you 'as it is' and in keeping with that I also have to tell you about just how cool it is to run your own business and be your own boss. It's brilliant.

It has taken nearly 20 years to get to where I am today. There are still very stressful moments but there are lots of people who would like to be where I am now. The bonus is, that because of the work and struggle of the journey, I have absolutely no problem enjoying the rewards of my labour. I have two properties, a couple of nice cars and a boat so that's not bad is it?

However, that is not the best bit for me. I really am proud of how I have earned my money. I am not a slum landlord or worked in some finance business taking a cut of other people's money. I have made something I am proud to put my name to and I personally feel it is great to be in manufacturing. Showing people around the company's factory and meeting the team here brings me joy every time I do it. Do not get me wrong, posh season tickets for the football, fantastic holidays and spoiling my kids also helps bring joy!

Sometimes, it does trouble me that it is all people see now, but like I said, I know where the money is from and my true friends know how hard I have worked and the risks I have taken. I try to always respect people and not abuse my 'boss' role, that's a top tip. Abusing responsibility is not a great attribute to have. I am also aware I have not got here alone. My wonderful sister who works within the business has kept me in check all my life and working with two fantastic partners has helped me. Together we have built a team and that is what has given me the freedom to take time off and enjoy the rewards.

I had a dark period after my parents died. I walked into the office one day and decided I needed to do something different, take some time out. That is when I started sailing. I took up a 'beginner to winner' sailing course and spent five months on the water. It was the first time I really felt the benefit of being my own boss. I am not sure if I would have had that opportunity had I not started this adventure back in 2003 and not had the support of my fellow directors. I am very grateful to them.

With no direct or formal management training, I am convinced that if you are bright and have the correct attitude to risk and work, anyone can achieve. You must have a little luck and select the right product/service to sell, but it is possible for anyone. The whole point of me writing all this stuff down is to give a real-life insight into the rewards of owning your own business and the shit that goes with it. Be very aware that just because you are a nice person and work hard does not mean you will be successful.

I cannot remember the last time I sat down for dinner at a normal restaurant and looked closely at the prices on the menu. I used to have to check my bank account daily. I am so proud of my children who use modern apps now to monitor their daily cash flow and expenditure. I am sure I would have achieved more if I was brighter. I am not a millionaire, my home is on an estate and not big but in comparison to where I am from, I have all I need, it is only now I realise my motivation is not money. It really is down to the fact that I am just quite driven and get bored easily, so it is important that I always have something to focus on. I am not a natural but I enjoy my work and early on realised what I was rubbish at, which gave me a clear view of what people I needed around me. If you can work that out, it is a great insight to how to plan your growth.

Meeting great people along the way is just amazing, the freedom to come and go as you please and to travel whenever and wherever makes it worth doing. The freedom should not be underestimated as it gives you the opportunity to spend time with the people you love. This is probably the biggest plus the job has given me. I think that it took ten years for me to get to that point. It was hand to mouth for the first three years but it is now paying back. There are periods when we have to keep things in check, a bad year can reduce the dividends (the joy of owning shares) and the money you subsequently get.

There definitely was a period where work had to come first but now the balance is the other way and it is nice. Having control is just amazing, the freedom to decide what happens when gets better with experience because the process of decision making becomes clearer.

Remember that nobody is ever going to see it from your angle, after all, you started it and it is your money but the ability to make the big call is lovely, stressful but lovely. What I do regard as a milestone was when I decided I did not want to work for a specific client. To walk away from work is not easy but now I have a choice and I like the ability to choose who we work for and with. I have only ever done this once by the way!

I have talked about flexible working hours but it does go hand in hand with positive habits and attributes that you need to demonstrate to your teams. I am talking about diligence, reliability, and punctuality. For years I was late to meetings and events simply because I always tried to fit in one more task or job before I got there but now I am always on time and prepared for each thing I do. Time is the most valuable thing to me now. I do sometimes over stretch myself and now and again need to be in two places at once but, hey, I am not perfect and I am surrounded by people that remind me of that!

Learning is another fantastic side effect of working for yourself. There is so much to take in. It is only when you start teaching others that you appreciate what you have learnt.

I am writing this at the tender age of 52. I cannot stop working yet as I still have a mortgage and bills to pay but to be in a position where you can think about stopping in the next ten years to enjoy retirement is exciting.

There is a certain degree of employment protection. I am so fortunate that I know I can work through a recession or downturn and the risk of losing my job is low. I did, however, get made redundant a couple of times during my early career and got fired once, that was not a nice experience. I do always try and put myself back there when I do have to ask people to leave.

Working with local schools is a passion of mine and working out ways to give back to the community has been rewarding. There are so many lovely things that go with the MD role, so always think forward to 'jam tomorrow' when you have tough times.

I like to think that my team trust me and I have empowered them but I do always feel self-aware and know that I should lead by example as much as I can. These are all good life skills that are a benefit of working for yourself. My mistakes are sometimes also so big that you can't miss them, I do still need to learn from them. Try to be humble and remember how lucky you are when things do fall in your favour.

Learn to adapt to things quickly – when the business started, and a friend asked me why I wanted to be my own boss, I could not really answer him. A year later, and I would have said something like, 'I have the ability to choose which 18 hours of a day I work'.

In reality, I just got fed up with what I was doing at the time and had definitely enough of my boss making money from all my efforts. I am so glad I decided to go for it. I was definitely nervous and had a fear of failure but I cracked on and had a go. If I lost it all now, I would be gutted but as my dad would say, "Well, you had a go. It's now time to get a proper job!"

There are lots of fluffy advantages to owning a business, getting invited to events, winning the odd business award and creating the working environment that you enjoy being in, they all matter in various degrees.

Making my dad proud of me was a nice thing to achieve and when we opened a new factory, I organised my father's hero, Lawrie McMenemy, a local long retired football manager, to open it and say a few words. He spent a full hour chatting to my dad which was priceless. It is not all about the bank balance, try to remember that.

I asked my family what they thought the plus side of having a Dad that runs a company. It was interesting and the first word was inheritance! That had to be my daughter, right. But more seriously, the children then went on to talk about the positives and negatives. There only seemed to be one negative, which was how many hours I worked in the early days, after that, they were able to point out lots of positives. They enjoy the stories I come back with and experiences I share with them that I am now sharing with you. They enjoy the boat. They have benefitted from work experience and they also enjoy the family days we organise for our employees which they get involved with to make sure everyone has fun.

Katie commented how I would turn things into a learning experience! I am surprised she regarded that as a positive, but her example was when we went to a furniture store and I pointed out an interesting drawer system. I made her video and send it to me so I could do some research! I think she felt a bit like a spy in the department store and she was learning about detailed design.

During my career, they have also met some interesting people from all over the world. We have had a BBQ at home with a Texan and a French Canadian just for starters. An old boss of mine used to say, "Not as queer as folk," which is a Northern English expression for how different people are. It is a joy for my kids to meet and get to know people from different backgrounds. It also means I have a huge network of people to talk to and learn from.

I remember my kids saying it is nice when people ask them what Dad does, and obviously, my ability to spoil them both from time to time just brings me joy as well as to them. I am very lucky and I hope when you take the same journey, it brings you joy during the journey and not just at the end.